MUSIC FOR HOLY WEEK & EASTER

A Music Resource

McCRIMMONS
Great Wakering Essex England

Contents

Palm Sunday

The Blessing of Palms 3
The Procession 9
The Liturgy of the Word 15

Maundy Thursday

The Liturgy of the Word 21
The Washing of Feet 29
The Liturgy of the Eucharist 38
The Procession of the Blessed Sacrament . . . 49

Good Friday

The Liturgy of the Word 54
The Veneration of the Cross 60

Easter Vigil

The Service of Light 118
The Liturgy of the Word 130
The Liturgy of Baptism 158

Easter Sunday

Easter Sunday 168
The Liturgy of the Word 171

* * *

Acknowledgements 192

Index of first lines and copyright owners 194

Liturgical index 196

Index of first lines 198

First published in the United Kingdom in 2001 by
MCCRIMMON PUBLISHING CO. LTD.
10-12 High Street, Great Wakering, Essex SS3 0EQ
Telephone 01702-218956 Fax 01702-216082
email: mccrimmons@dial.pipex.com
www.mccrimmons.com

Compilation and layout © 2001 McCrimmon Publishing Co. Ltd.

ISBN 085597 627 6
British Library Cataloguing in Publication Data.
A catalogue record for this book is available from the British Library.

Compiled by Joan McCrimmon and Elizabeth Upsher
Edited by Paul Davis

Music typesetting by Paul Davis and Stephen Dean
Cover design by Nick Snode
Printed and bound by Thanet Press Ltd, Margate, Kent

Palm Sunday

THE BLESSING OF PALMS

When the people have assembled, the antiphon 'Hosanna' is sung.

First Setting

Stephen Dean

Each phrase is sung by a Cantor (or a group of the choir) and repeated by all (led by the rest of the choir)

Ho - san-na to the Son of Da - vid! The King of Is - ra - el!

Bles - sed is he who comes in the name of the Lord! Lord! Ho - san - na in the

high - est! Ho - san - na in the high - est! Ho san - na in the - high - est heavens!

Second Setting

Tony Barr

The refrain is sung after each verse. The harmony is optional.

Cantor:

(instruments)

Ho - san - na, ho - san-na, ho - san -

All (alto line is melody)

na! Ho - san - na, ho - san - na, ho - san - na!

Verses (melody line in lower stave)

1. Ho - san - na to the Son of Da - vid! Ho - san - na to the King! Ho -
2. Blest be the One who comes in the name of the Lord! Blest

san - na to the Son of Da - vid, the King of Is - ra - el. **Ho -**
be the One who in the Lord's name is co - ming here this day.

Third Setting

Sir Richard R Terry
(1865-1938)

(Originally a tone higher.)

Fourth Setting

Kevin Mayhew

Unison or SATB

Ho - san - na to the Son of Da - vid,_____ the King of Is - ra

the King

the King

el. Bles - sed is he who comes_ in the name of the

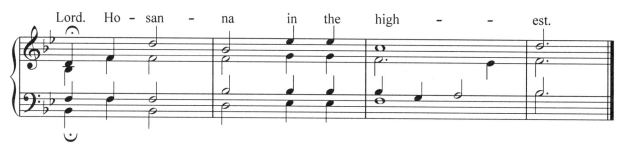

Lord. Ho - san - na in the high - - est.

Fifth Setting

Kevin Mayhew

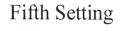

Unison

Ho - san - na to the Son of Da - vid,_ the King of Is - ra - el. Bles - sed is

he who comes in the name of the Lord. Ho - san - na - in_ the_ high - est.

For information on copyright, see acknowledgements page

Sixth Setting

John Rombaut

Seventh Setting

Also suitable during the Procession.
The refrain may be sung in canon.

Jaques Berthier (1923-1994)

Ho - san - na, ho - san - na, ho - san - na in ex - cel - sis. Ho-

Keyboard

Choir

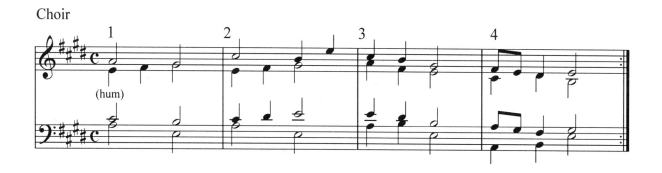

(hum)

Guitar

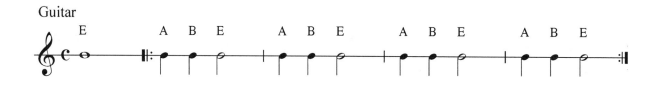

Soprano or Instrument

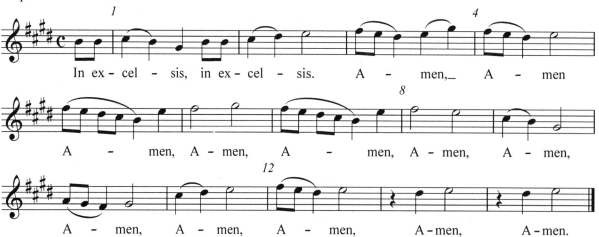

In ex - cel - sis, in ex - cel - sis. A - men,__ A - men

A - men, A - men, A - men, A - men, A - men,

A - men, A - men, A - men, A - men, A - men.

THE PROCESSION

Songs during the procession

All Glory, Laud and Honour

ST THEODULPH 7676 D

Melchior Teschner 1615

Chorus:
**All glory, laud and honour
to thee, Redeemer, King,
to whom the lips of children
made sweet Hosannas ring.**

1 Thou art the King of Israel,
   thou David's royal Son,
   who in the Lord's name comest,
   the King and blessed one.

2 The company of angels
   are praising thee on high,
   and mortal folk, with all things
   created, make reply.

3 The people of the Hebrews
   with palms before thee went:
   our praise and prayer and anthems
   before thee we present.

4 To thee before thy Passion
   they sang their hymns of praise;
   to thee now high exalted
   our melody we raise.

5 Thou didst accept their praises,
   accept the prayers we bring,
   who in all good delightest,
   thou good and gracious king.

*St Theodulph of Orleans (d821)
tr. John Mason Neale (1818-1866)*

The Children of Jerusalem

Dom Gregory Murray

Psalm 23

1. The Lord's is the earth <u>and</u> it's fulness,
   the world and <u>all</u> it's peoples.
   It is he who set it <u>on</u> the seas
   on the waters he <u>made</u> it firm.

2. Who shall climb the mountain <u>of</u> the Lord?
   Who shall stand in his <u>holy</u> place?
   The man with clean hands and pure heart,
   who desires not <u>worth</u>less things,
   who has not sworn so as to de<u>ceive</u> his neighbour.

3. He shall receive blessings <u>from</u> the Lord
   and reward from the <u>God</u> who saves him.
   Such are the <u>men</u> who seek him,
   seek the face of the <u>God</u> of Jacob.

4. O gates, lift high your heads;
   grow higher, <u>ancient</u> doors.
   Let him enter, the <u>king</u> of glory!

5. Who is the king of glory?
   The Lord, the <u>mighty</u>, the valiant,
   the Lord, the <u>valiant</u> in war.

6. O gates, lift high your heads;
   grow higher <u>ancient</u> doors,
   Let him enter, the <u>king</u> of glory!

7. Who is he, the king of glory?
   He, the <u>Lord</u> of armies,
   he is the <u>king</u> of glory.

For information on copyright, see acknowledgements page

Come to Jerusalem

Israeli Folksong

Chorus

Come to Je-ru-sa-lem, re-joi-cing be-fore him!

Greet him with loud ho-san-nas, bow down, a-dore him!

Verses

1. All peo-ples, clap your hands, cry out to your ma-ker!
2. God mounts the throne with joy, with bla-ring of trum-pets!
3. God is the king of all the na-tions, O praise him!
4. Peo-ples and prin-ces come in ho-mage to meet him.

God is the Lord of all, O trem-ble be-fore him!
Sing praise to God Al-migh-ty, king of the na-tions!
Praise him with all your skill, en-throned in his tem-ple!
God is the migh-ty one, the world is his king-dom!

Ps 47(46), adapted by Stephen Dean

When the people heard

As the procession enters the church, the following antiphon may be sung.
The congregation could be encouraged to join in at 'Hosanna in the highest'.

Dom Gregory Murray

Unison or SATB: When the peo-ple heard that Je-sus was en-ter-ing Je-ru-sa-lem, they went to meet him, and wa-ving o-live bran-ches they loud-ly praised the Lord: Ho-san-na in the high-est.

Chosen People of the Lord

St Benedict's Farm

Lord, strong and migh - ty, the Lord of vic-to - ry.
Lord, he is co - ming to stay for e - ver- more.
Lord great and migh - ty, the Lord, the Lord is King.

Bm   F#   Bm   F#   Bm   A7

Pueri Hebraeorum

This Antiphon may be used alone, or sung between the
verses of Psalm 23 (text on page 10) with a suitable Psalm tone.

Plainsong
Accomp. Paul Davis

Pu - e - ri Heb - rae - o - rum, *por- tan - tes ra - mos o - li - va - rum,

ob - vi - a - ve - runt Do - mi - no,

cla - man - tes, et di - cen - tes: Ho - san - na in ex - cel - sis.

Lauda Jerusalem

Th. Deckers

Response

Lau-da, Je-ru-sa-lem, Do - mi-num. Lau-da-De-um tu-um Zi - on.

Ho - san - na! Ho - san - na! Ho-san-na fi-li-o___ Da - vid!

Fine

Verses

1. O praise the   Lord,   Je - ru - sa - lem!
2. He has strengthened the   bars   of   your   gates,
3. He has established   peace   on   your   borders,
4. He sends out his   word   to   the   earth
5. He showers down   snow   white   as   wool,
6. He hurls down   hail - - stones   like   crumbs.
7. He sends forth his   word   and   it   melts them:
8. He makes his   word   known   to   Jacob,
9. He has not dealt thus with   o - - ther   nations;

1. O Zion, sing   praise   to   your   God!
2. he has blessed the   child - - ren   with - in you
3. he feeds you with   fi - - nest   wheat.
4. and swiftly   runs   his   com - mand.
5. he scatters   hoar - frost   like   ashes.
6. The waters are   fro - zen   at   his   touch.
7. at the breath of his   mouth   the   wa - ters   flow.
8. to Israel his   laws   and   de - crees.
9. he has not taught them   his   de - - crees.

D.C.

Psalm 147, Grail translation

THE LITURGY OF THE WORD

RESPONSORIAL PSALM

First Setting

Anthony Milner

Unison

My God, my God, why have you for - sa - ken me?

1. All who see me de- ride me. They curl their
2. Many dogs have sur - rounded me; A
3. They di - vide my clothing a- mong them.
4. I will tell of your name to my brethren, and

1. lips, they toss their heads. 'He trusted in the
2. band of the wicked be - set me. They tear holes in my
3. They cast lots for my robe. O Lord, do not
4. praise you where they are as - sembled. You who fear the
   *all sons of

1. Lord, let him save him, let him re - lease him if this is his friend.'
2. hands and my feet. I can count eve - ry one of my bones.
3. leave me a- lone; my strength, make haste to help me.
4. Lord, give him praise, *(return to *)* Re- vere him, Isra - el's sons.
   Jacob, give him glory.

Second Setting

Peter Laugier

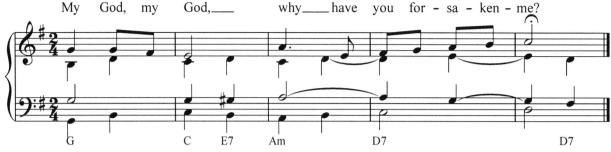
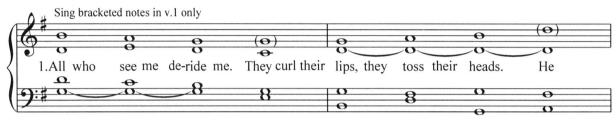
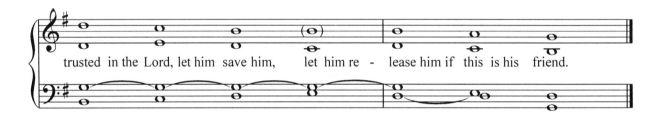

2. Many <u>dogs</u> have sur<u>rou</u>nded me,
   a <u>band</u> of the <u>wicked</u> be<u>set</u> me.
   They tear <u>holes</u> in my <u>hands</u> and my <u>feet</u>,
   I can <u>count</u> every <u>one</u> of my <u>bones</u>.

3. They di<u>vide</u> my <u>clothing</u> a<u>mong</u> them,
   they <u>cast</u> <u>lots</u> for my <u>robe</u>.
   O <u>Lord</u>, do not <u>leave</u> me a<u>lone</u>,
   my <u>strength</u>, make <u>haste</u> to <u>help</u> me!

4. I will <u>tell</u> of your <u>name</u> to my <u>brethren</u>,
   and <u>praise</u> you where <u>they</u> are as<u>sem</u>bled.
   You who <u>fear</u> the <u>Lord</u>, give him <u>praise</u>;
   re<u>vere</u> him, Israel's <u>sons</u>.

Third Setting

Paul Davis

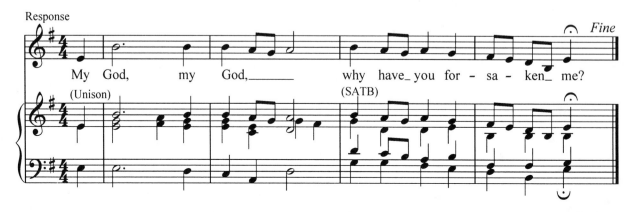

Loreto Tone 6,
adapted by Paul Davis

Fourth Setting

Anne Ward

For information on copyright, see acknowledgements page

GOSPEL ACCLAMATION
First Setting

Stephen Dean

The response is sung between verses.

Verses *(sung by cantor or choir with response between)*

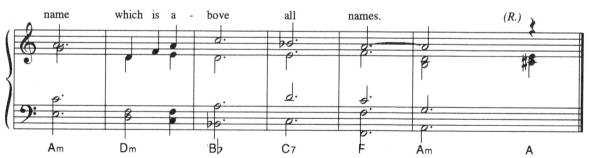

Second Setting

John Lillis

Each phrase is sung by a cantor or choir and repeated by all.

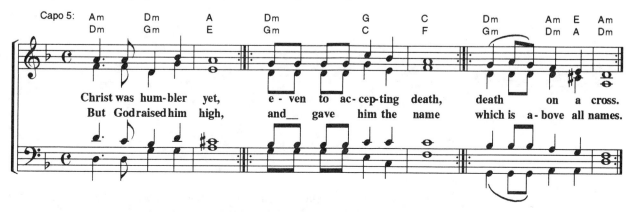

Third Setting

Ian Coleman

Praise to you, O Christ, King of e - ter - nal glo ry!

Christ was hum - bler yet, even to accep - ting death, death on a cross.

But God raised him high, and gave to him the name which is a - bove all names.

Though one with God

JERUSALEM (DLM)

C.H.H.Parry (1848-1918)

1. Though one with God, yet not by might did Christ his e - qual sta - tus
2. There - fore God raised him af - ter death, raised him to reign in earth and

claim: in - stead he gave up all he had and as a hum - ble ser - vant
heaven: The one who we con - si - dered least, the grea - test name by God was

came. In world - ly form, of wo - man born, he lived at one with hu - man -
given. And so, to ho - nour Je - sus' name, all who have life or are to

kind, and strode and stum - bled to the cross that we the path to life might find.
be shall kneel pro - clai - ming 'Christ is Lord!' and wor - ship God e - ter - nal - ly.

Philippians 2:6-11, versified by John Bell and Graham Maule.

Maundy Thursday

EVENING MASS OF THE LORD'S SUPPER

THE LITURGY OF THE WORD

Entrance Song

WAREHAM (LM)

Later form of a melody by William Knapp (1698-1768)
first found in *A Sett of New Psalm Tunes & Anthems* (1738)

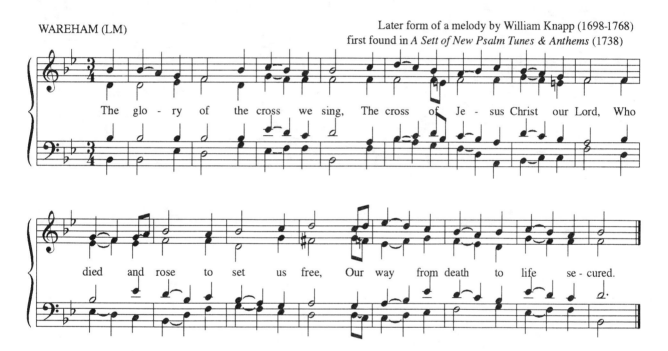

The glo-ry of the cross we sing, The cross of Je-sus Christ our Lord, Who died and rose to set us free, Our way from death to life se-cured.

2. As once God's people rested safe,
   Protected by a lamb's own blood,
   So we acclaim the sacrifice
   Of Jesus Christ the Lamb of God.

3. As once the Chosen People passed
   From pain to freedom through the sea,
   So now baptismal water saves
   The chosen, called to liberty.

4. At passover before he died
   Christ Jesus took the bread and wine:
   'This is my body, this my blood,
   Do this as my memorial sign.'

5. What once by Jesus was achieved
   We celebrate with heart and soul,
   Recalling and effecting now
   The saving work that makes us whole.

John Ainslie

RESPONSORIAL PSALM
First Setting

Stephen Dean

For information on copyright, see acknowledgements page

VERSES 2 & 3 (accompaniment as for v.1)

(Christ) 2. O pre-cious in the eyes of the Lord is the death of his

(Christ). 3. A thanks - gi-ving sa-cri-fice I make, I will call on the

faith - ful. Your ser - vant, Lord, your ser - vant am I; you have loo - sened my

Lord: my vows to the Lord I will ful - fil be - fore all his

bonds. R.Our

peo - ple. R.Our

Second Setting

A. Gregory Murray O.S.B.

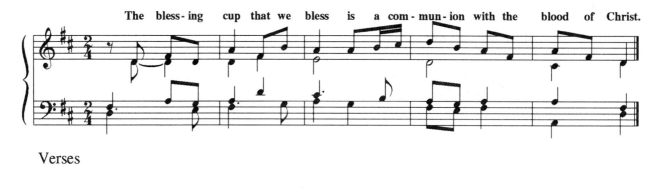

Verses

1. How can I repay the Lord
   for his goodness to me?
   The cup of salvation I will raise;
   I will call on the Lord's name.

2. O precious in the eyes of the Lord
   is the death of his faithful.
   Your servant, Lord, your servant am I;
   you have loosened my bonds.

3. A thanksgiving sacrifice I make:
   I will call on the Lord's name.
   My vows to the Lord I will fulfil
   before all his people.

Third Setting

Paul Davis

Response: The bles-sing cup that we bless_____ is a com-mu-nion with the blood of Christ.

Fine

Verses (Without a fixed beat)

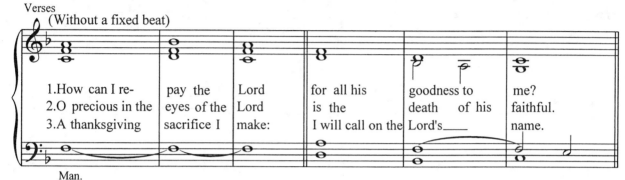

1. How can I re- | pay the | Lord | for all his | goodness to | me?
2. O precious in the | eyes of the | Lord | is the | death of his | faithful.
3. A thanksgiving | sacrifice I | make: | I will call on the | Lord's____ | name.

Man.

(Resume the beat)   D.C.

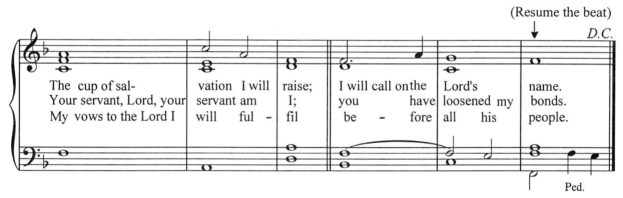

The cup of sal- | vation I will | raise; | I will call on the | Lord's | name.
Your servant, Lord, your | servant am | I; | you | have loosened my | bonds.
My vows to the Lord I | will ful - | fil | be - fore | all his | people.

Ped.

Fourth Setting

Garfield Rochard

Response

D   G   A7   D

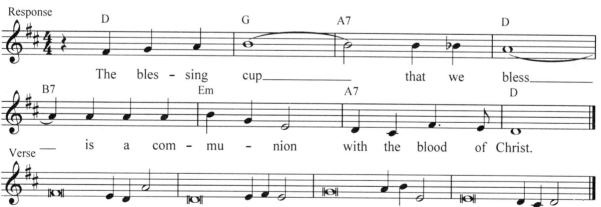

The bles - sing cup_____ that we bless_____

B7   Em   A7   D

Verse —— is a com - mu - nion with the blood of Christ.

1. How can I repay the Lord
   for his goodness to me?
   The cup of salvation I will raise;
   I will call on the Lord's name.

2. O precious in the eyes of the Lord
   is the death of his faithful.
   Your servant, Lord, your servant am I
   you have loosened my bonds.

3. A thanksgiving sacrifice I make
   I will call on the Lord's name.
   My vows to the Lord I will fulfill
   before all his people.

Fifth Setting

Christopher Walker

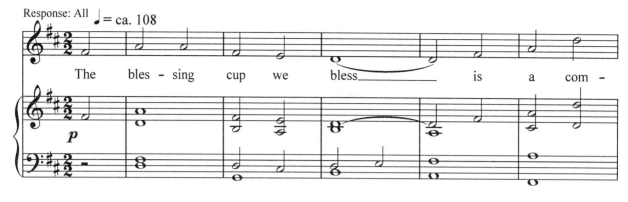

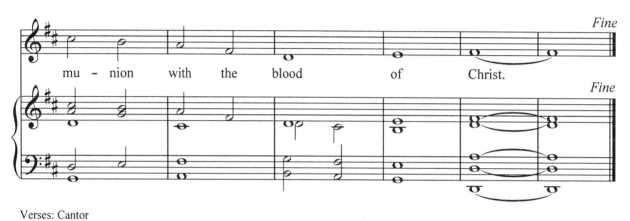

Verses: Cantor

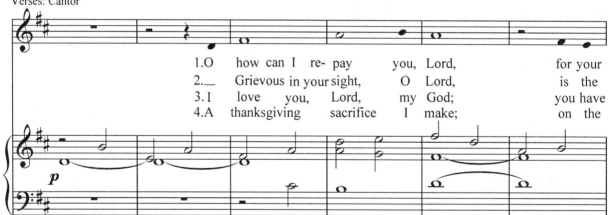

1. O how can I re- pay you, Lord, for your
2. ___ Grievous in your sight, O Lord, is the
3. I love you, Lord, my God; you have
4. A thanksgiving sacrifice I make; on the

good - ness to me? I will raise the cup of sal
death of your faithful. O___ Lord, I am your
heard the cry of my dis- tress. I will call to you as long as I
Lord's name I will call. I will carry out my vows to the

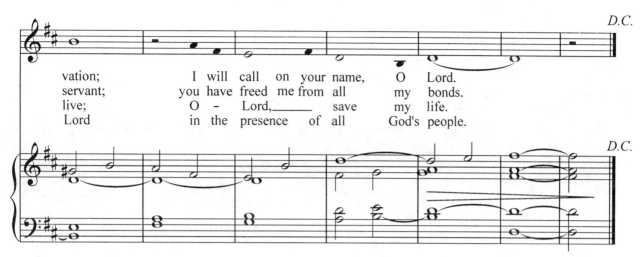

vation;   I will call on your name,   O   Lord.
servant;   you have freed me from all   my   bonds.
live;   O – Lord,_____ save   my   life.
Lord   in the presence of all   God's people.

GOSPEL ACCLAMATION
First Setting

Stephen Dean

Introduction: *Vigorous* ♩=66   ℅ Refrain: *Cantor/Choir then All*

Praise and ho - nour to you, praise and ho - nour to you, Lord Je - sus!

Verse (Cantor or choir)

Much slower

I give you a new commandment: Love one a - no - ther, just as

I have loved you. *tempo primo* ℅

Second Setting

Chris O'Hara

Glo - ry and praise to you, Lord, you are the Word of Life. A new command - ment I give you, says the Lord. Love one a - no - ther just as I have loved you.

Third Setting

Garfield Rochard

Je - sus, you are the word of God, the li - ving Word of God, Je - sus you're Lord. A new com - mand - ment I leave you: love one a - no - ther as I have loved you.

Fourth Setting

Kevin Mayhew

Unison or SATB

I give you a new com - mand - ment:

I give you a new com - mand - ment

Love__ one a - no - ther as I have loved__ you.

THE WASHING OF FEET

During this rite, hymns and songs may be sung. The following are suggested:

The Lord Jesus, when he had eaten

Dom Gregory Murray

Unison or SATB

pp

The Lord Je - sus, when he had ea - ten with his dis - ci - ples, poured

cresc. *3* *mf* *cresc.*

wa - ter in - to a ba - sin, and be - gan to wash__ their__

dim. *p* *pp*

feet,__ say - ing: This ex - am - ple I leave__ you.

The Lord Jesus
Introduction

Gregory Norbet
Words from St John

The Lord Je-sus, af-ter ea-ting with his friends, washed their feet and said to them: Do you know what I, your Lord, have done to you? I have gi-ven you ex-am-ple, that so you al-so should do.

For information on copyright, see acknowledgements page

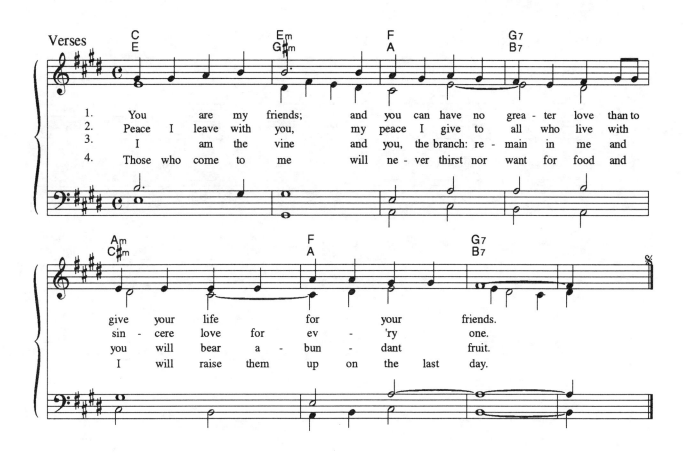

Verses

1. You are my friends; and you can have no grea - ter love than to
2. Peace I leave with you, my peace I give to all who live with
3. I am the vine and you, the branch: re - main in me and
4. Those who come to me will ne - ver thirst nor want for food and

give your life for your friends.
sin - cere love for ev - 'ry one.
you will bear a - bun - dant fruit.
I will raise them up on the last day.

Instrumental descant for verse

A New Commandment

Melody: anonymous
Arr: McCrimmons

2 You are my friends if you do what I command you.
   Without my help you can do nothing. *(Repeat)*

3 I am the true vine, my Father is the gard'ner.
   Abide in me: I will be with you. *(Repeat)*

4 True love is patient, not arrogant or boastful;
   love bears all things, love is eternal. *(Repeat)*

Text: v1 John 13; vv 2-4 Aniceto Nazareth
based on John 15 and 1 Corinthians 13

Lord, do you wash my feet?

Paschal Jordan

Lord, do you wash my feet? Je-sus said to him: If I do not wash your feet, you can

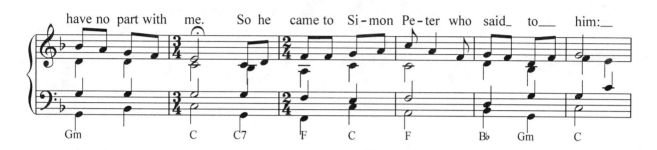

have no part with me. So he came to Si-mon Pe-ter who said_ to_ him:_

Lord, do you wash my feet? Now you do not know what I am do-ing,_ but

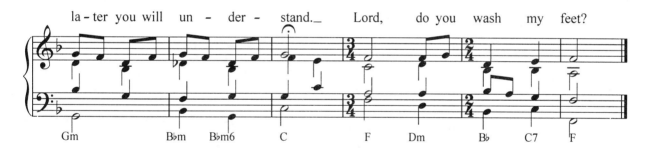

la-ter you will un - der - stand._ Lord, do you wash my feet?

No Greater Love

Michael Joncas

keep my commands, ev- en as I have kept my Fa - ther's.

I have loved you: this is my com - mand.

I have made known to you: Now I call you friends.

you will re - ceive all you ask the Fa- ther in my name.

FINAL REFRAIN

Sopranos:

Altos:

No grea - ter, grea - ter love than to lay down, lay

Basses and Assembly:

There is no grea-ter love, says the Lord, than to lay down your life for a

THE LITURGY OF THE EUCHARIST

*During the **Procession of Gifts** the* Ubi Caritas *is sung.*

Ostinato Response

Jacques Berthier

Accompaniments: Keyboard

Guitar

Cello

For information on copyright, see acknowledgements page

Verses: Cantor

1. Your love, O Jesus Christ, has gathered us together.

2. May your love, O Jesus Christ, be foremost in our lives.

3. Let us love one another as God has loved us.
*Choose either part.

4. Let us be one in love together in the one bread of Christ.

5. The love of God in Jesus Christ bears eternal joy.

6. The love of God in Jesus Christ will never have an end.

Where is love

Alan Rees, O.S.B.

Refrain

Where is love and lo-ving-kind - ness, God is there.

Verses (cantor)

1. The love of Christ has gathered us to-ge-ther in one: let us then re-joice and be glad in him.

2. Let us fear and love the li-ving God; let us love each o-ther from the depths of our hearts.

3. Therefore when we are to-ge - ther let us take heed not to be di-vi-ded in mind.

4. Let there be an end to bi-ter-ness and quar rels, an end to strife, and in our midst be Christ our God.

5. And in com-pa-ny with the bles - sed may we see your face in glo - ry, Christ our God: pure and un-boun - ded joy for e - ver and e - ver. A - men.

For information on copyright, see acknowledgements page

Ubi caritas

Plainsong
Accompaniment: Paul Davis

Refrain

U-bi ca - ri - tas et a - mor,_ De-us i - bi est.
(or: *est ve - ra__*)

1. Con - gre - ga - vit_ nos in u -
2. Si - mul er - go_ cum in u -
3. Si - mul quo - que_ cum be - a -

num_ Chris-ti a - mor. Ex-sul-te - mus_ et in ip - so_ iu - cun-de-mur.
num_ con - gre - ga - mur: ne nos men - te_ di - vi - da - mus,_ ca - ve - a-mus.
-tis_ vi - de - a - mus glo - ri - an - ter_ vul-tum tu - um, Chris-te De - us:

Ti - me - a - mus_ et a - me - mus_ De - um vi - vum.
Ces-sent iur - gi - a ma - lig - na,_ ces - sent li - tes.
gau - di - um quod_ est im - men - sum,_ at - que pro-bum,

Et ex cor - de_ di - li - ga - mus_ nos sin - ce - ro.
Et in me - di - o nos-tri_ sit_ Chris - tus_ De - us.
sae - cu - la per_ in - fi - ni - ta_ sae - cu - lo - rum.

Broken for me

Janet Lunt

For information on copyright, see acknowledgements page

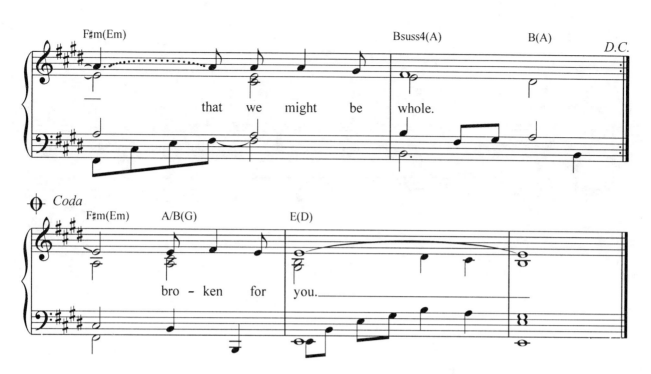

that we might be whole.

Coda

bro – ken for you.

2. This is My body given for you;
   Eat it remembering I died for you.

3. This is My blood I shed for you,
   For your forgiveness, making you new.

Eat this bread

Jaques Berthier (1923-1994)

Eat this bread, drink this cup, come to me and ne – ver be hun – gry.

Eat this bread, drink this cup, trust in me and you will not thirst.

Keyboard or guitar

G C Am D Bm Em D G D Em Bm C D G

Communion meditation

Canon in two parts, repeated ad libitum

Stephen Dean

Fa - ther,__ if this cup may not pass me by__ but I must drink it;

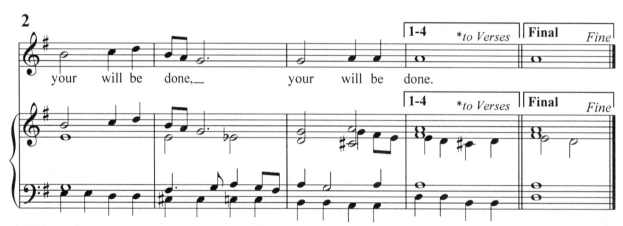

your will be done,__ your will be done.

* If the Refrain is sung as a canon, repeat the accompaniment from 2

1. With - out__ beau - ty, with - out ma - jes - ty we
2. This is my ser - vant; he will be
3. We thought him pu - nished, struck down__ and af-
4. Though he was fault - less, the Lord God let him

saw__ him,__   a man of sor - rows,   des - pised and re-
lif - ted high,__   kings of the earth__   stand speech - less be-
flic - ted by God;   yet ours the sor - rows,   ours were the
suf - fer,__   he was made vic - tim,   his life an a-

jec - ted.   As__ one from whom peo - ple hide their fa - ces,
fore__ him.   So dis - fi - gured, he seemed no long - er hu - man,
griefs he bore.   For our sins he was pierced__ and woun - ded,
tone - ment.   By his an - guish shall ma - ny be made right - teous,

he was brought low   and we heed -ed him not.
in him the pow'r   of the Lord is re - vealed.
and through his suf - frings_ we are made whole.
his im - mo - la - tion will wipe out our sins.

The Bread that we break

Stephen Dean

Introduction (first time only)

Refrain

The bread that we break is a sha - ring in Christ's

bo - dy; the cup that we bless, a com - mun - ion in his blood.

Verses

1. Christ the Lord, on the night he was be - trayed, took the
2. For as of - ten as you shall break the bread and shall
3. For as there is one bread, we though ma - ny are
4. So we thank you that we are coun - ted wor - thy to
5. And may we who have shared in his bo - dy and

bread and blessed the cup, say-ing: 'Do this, my friends, in re-
drink this cup, you pro-claim the Lord's death, till he
one in him, like the wheat once scat-tered that
stand be-fore you and to serve at this ta-ble from
in his sa-ving blood, be u-nited in the Spi-rit who

mem-br'ance of me.'
comes a-gain.
makes the one bread. **The**
which we are fed.
gives us life.

D.S.

Bread of the world

Je suis le maitre 9898

17th Century French Carol
arr. Paul Davis

1. Bread of the world in mercy broken,
   Wine of the soul in sorrow shed,
   By whom the words of life were spoken,
   And in whose death our sins are dead:

2. Look on the heart by sorrow broken,
   Look on the tears by sinners shed,
   And be thy feast to us the token
   That by thy grace our souls are fed.

Reginald Heber 1783-1826

Come, Christ's beloved

James Walsh, O.S.B.
arr. by Anthony Greening

Refrain

1. Come, Christ's be - lo - ved, feed__ on Christ's true flesh,
3. Christ, in this mys - t'ry gives__ his flesh and blood,
5. Christ, priest and vic - tim, gave__ him - self for all,
7. Christ, our sal - va - tion, Christ the light of all,
*12. Come, Christ's be - lo - ved, feed__ on Christ's true flesh,

However many verses are sung, always conclude with this one.

fine

Drink your re - demp - tion in his pre - cious blood.
Gui - ding us safe - ly through death's gates to life.
At once the gi - ver and his gift di - vine.
has yet en - riched us by this gift sub - lime.
Drink your re - demp - tion in his pre - cious blood.

Verses

2. Here is sal - va - tion, here, the ri - sen Lord, Here
4. Son of the Fa - ther, Lord of all the world, Christ
6. Priests of the old law, off - 'ring blood out - poured, Did
8. Bring to his ban - quet faith - ful hearts sin - cere, Take

God's great ban - quet: let us thank our God.
is our Sa - viour thro' his Cross - and blood.
but fore - sha - dow Christ, the vic - tim priest.
now the safe - guard of e - ter - nal life.

From the Bangor Antiphonary, (c.7), tr. James Quinn, S.J., alt.

9. Christ, ever-watchful shepherd of his sheep, gives true belivers life that knows no end.

10. Christ gives the hungry heavn'ly bread to eat; he gives the thirst living springs of grace.

11. Alpha, the firstborn, Omega, our end; you came as Saviour, you will come as judge.

THE PROCESSION OF THE BLESSED SACRAMENT

Of the glorious body telling

First Tune

ST THOMAS (87 87 87)

Possibly by J.F.Wade (1711-1786)

1.Of the glo-rious bo-dy tel-ling, O my tongue, its mys-teries sing,

and the blood, all price ex-cell-ing, which the world's ter-nal king,

in a no-ble womb once dwel-ling, shed for this world's ran-som-ing.

2 Given for us, for us descending,
of a virgin to proceed,
Man with man in converse blending
Scattered he the Gospel seed;
Till his sojourn drew to ending,
Which he closed in wondrous deed.

3 At the last great supper lying
Circled by his brethren's band,
Meekly with the law complying,
First he finished its command,
Then, immortal food supplying,
Gave himself with his own hand.

4 Word made flesh, by word he maketh
Very bread his flesh to be;
Man in wine Christ's blood partaketh;
And if senses fail to see,
Faith alone the true heart waketh
To behold the mystery.

5 Therefore we, béfore him bending,
This great sacrament revere;
Types and shadows have their ending,
For the newer rite is here;
Faith, our outward sense befriending,
Makes the inward vision clear.

6 Glory let us give, and blessing
To the Father and the Son;
Honour, might and and praise addressing,

While eternal ages run;
Ever too his love confessing,
Who, from both, with both is one.

Attrib. St Thomas Aquinas (1227-1274), Tr. J. M. Neale, Edward Caswall et al.

Second Tune

PICARDY (87 87 87)

French Carol Tune

1 Of the glorious body telling,
  O my tongue, its mysteries sing,
  And the blood, all price excelling,
  Which the world's eternal king,
  In a noble womb once dwelling,
  Shed for this world's ransoming.

2 Given for us, for us descending,
  of a virgin to proceed,
  Man with man in converse blending
  Scattered he the Gospel seed,
  Till his sojourn drew to ending,
  Which he closed in wondrous deed.

3 At the last great supper lying
  Circled by his brethren's band,
  Meekly with the law complying,
  First he finished its command,
  Then, immortal food supplying,
  Gave himself with his own hand.

4 Word made flesh, by word he maketh
  Very bread his flesh to be;
  Man in wine Christ's blood partaketh;
  And if senses fail to see,
  Faith alone the true heart waketh
  To behold the mystery.

5 Therefore we, before him bending,
  This great sacrament revere;
  Types and shadows have their ending,
  For the newer rite is here;
  Faith, our outward sense befriending,
  Makes the inward vision clear.

6 Glory let us give, and blessing
  To the Father and the Son;
  Honour, might and and praise addressing,
  While eternal ages run;
  Ever too his love confessing,
  Who, from both, with both is one.

Attrib. St Thomas Aquinas (1227-1274)
Tr. J. M. Neale, Edward Caswall et al.

Pange Lingua (original version)

Plainsong, arr. A.G.M.

1.Pan-ge lin-gua glo-ri-o-si Cor-po-ris my-ste-ri-um,

San-gui-nis-que pre-ti-o-si Quem in mun-di pre-ti-um

Fruc-tus ven-tris ge-ne-ro-si Rex ef-fu-dit gen-ti-um. A-men.

2. Nobis datus, nobis natus
   ex intacta Virgine;
   et in mundo conversatus
   sparso verbi semine,
   sui moras incolatus
   miro clausit ordine.

3. In supremae noctae coenae
   recumbens cum fratribus,
   observata lege plene
   cibis in legalibus:
   cibum turbae duodenae
   se dat suis manibus.

4. Verbum caro, panem verum
   Verbo carnem efficit:
   fitque sanguis Christi merum;
   et si sensus deficit
   ad firmandum cor sincerum
   sola fides sufficit.

5. Tantum ergo sacramentum
   veneremur cernui;
   et antiquum documentum
   novo cedat ritui:
   praestet fides supplementum
   sensuum defectui.

6. Genitori, genitoque
   laus et jubilatio,
   salus, honor, virtus quoque
   sit et benedictio:
   procedenti ab utroque
   compar sit laudatio. Amen.

During the watching

My soul is sad

Words & music: Francesca Leftley

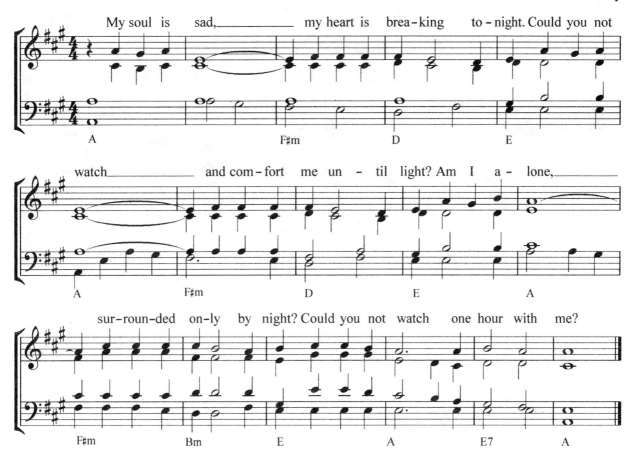

2. Could you not keep awake for one hour with me?
   Is it so hard that you should do this for me?
   I die for you that you might always be free.
   Could you not watch one hour with me?

3. And so I weep, and there is no one to hear,
   I am in pain; will no one witness my tears?
   I am your God, and as my Passion draws near,
   could you not watch one hour with me?

Stay here and keep watch

Jaques Berthier (1923-1994)
Words from Matthew 26, by Taizé

Good Friday

CELEBRATION OF THE LORD'S PASSION

PART ONE: THE LITURGY OF THE WORD

RESPONSORIAL PSALM
First Setting

Psalm 30: 2, 6, 12-13, 15-17, 25 R. Luke 23:46
A. Gregory Murray, O.S.B.

1. In you, O Lord, I take refuge;
   let me never be <u>put</u> to shame.
   In your justice, <u>set</u> me free.
   Into your hands I com<u>mend</u> my spirit.
   It is you who will re-<u>deem</u> me, Lord.

2. In the face of <u>all</u> my foes
   I am <u>a</u> reproach,
   an object of scorn <u>to</u> my neighbours
   and of fear <u>to</u> my friends.

3. Those who see me <u>in</u> the street
   run <u>far</u> away from me.
   I am like a dead man, forgotten <u>in</u> men's hearts,
   like a thing th<u>rown</u> away.

4. But as for me, I trust <u>in</u> you, Lord,
   I say: 'You <u>are</u> my God.
   My life is in your <u>hands</u>, deliver me
   from the hands of <u>all</u> who hate me.'

5. 'Let your face shine <u>on</u> your servant.
   Save me <u>in</u> your love.'
   Be strong, let your h<u>eart</u> take courage,
   all who hope <u>in</u> the Lord.'

Second Setting

Stephen Dean

Refrain (unaccompanied)

Slow ♩ = 60

Verse

Text of Psalm as for previous setting.

Third Setting

Fiona Macardle

Ostinato Response

The assembly is divided into two sections (two parts of the congregation, or congregation/choir, or all/
instruments). Section 1 begins at A and section 2 at B. The response is sung continuously while the cantor
adds the verses.

In - to your hands,   O Lord,   I com - mend   my   spi - rit.

Verses (Cantor)

1. Be a rock   of re - fuge for me, a migh-ty strong - hold to save   me, you are my rock;   for your name's sake,   lead and guide   me.

2. In - to your hands I com-mend my   spi-rit, it is You   who will re - deem   me, Lord.   As for me,   I trust   in the Lord,   I re - joice   in your love.

3. Let your face   shine   on your ser - vant;   Save   me   in your love.   You hide us in the shel-ter of your pre - sence,   from the plot-ting   of men.

Fourth Setting

Paschal Jordan

1. In you, O Lord, I take refuge.
   Let me never be put to shame.
   In your justice, set me free.
   Into your hands I commend my spirit;
   it is you who will redeem me, Lord.

2. In the face of all my foes
   I am a reproach,
   an object of scorn to my neighbours
   and of fear to my friends.

3. Those who see me in the streets
   run far away from me.
   I am like a dead man, forgotten in men's hearts,
   like a thing thrown away.

4. But as for me, I trust in you, Lord,
   I say: You are my God.
   My life is in your hands,
   deliver me from the hands of those who hate me.

5. Let your face shine on on your servant.
   Save me in your love.
   Be strong, let your heart take courage,
   all who hope in the Lord.

Fifth Setting

Ian Coleman

For information on copyright, see acknowledgements page

1. In you, O Lord, I take refuge.
   Let me never be put to shame.
   In your justice, set me free.
   Into your hands I commend my spirit.
   It is you who will redeem me, Lord.

2. In the face of all my foes
   I am a reproach,
   an object of scorn to my neighbours
   and of fear to my friends.

3. Those who see me in the street
   run far away from me.
   I am like a dead man, forgotten in men's hearts,
   like a thing thrown away.

4. But as for me, I trust in you, Lord,
   I say: 'You are my God.'
   My life is in your hands,
   deliver me from the hands of those who hate me.

5. Let your face shine on your servant.
   Save me in your love.
   Be strong, let your heart take courage,
   all who hope in the Lord.

GOSPEL ACCLAMATION

First Setting

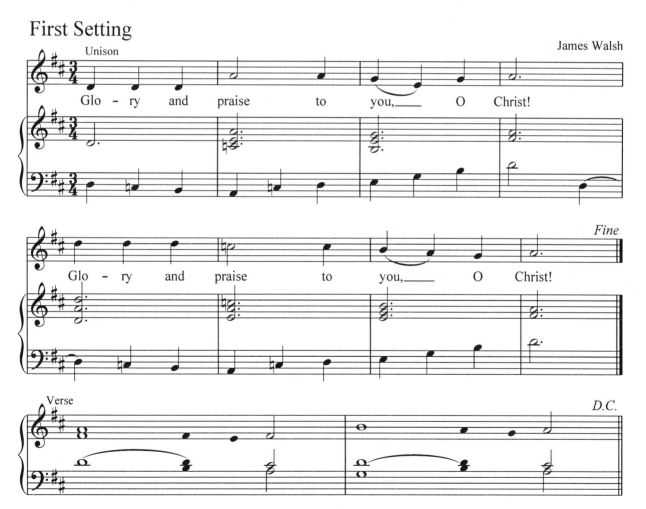

Glo-ry and praise to you,___ O Christ!

Glo-ry and praise to you,___ O Christ!

Christ was humbler yet,
even to accepting death, death on a cross,
But God raised him high
and gave him the name which is above all names.

Phil 2:8-9

GOSPEL ACCLAMATION

Second Setting

Refrain

1. Cantor; 2. All (+SATB)

Tony Barr

Praise to you, Lord Je - sus Christ, King of end - less glo - ry.

Verse (cantor/choir)

Christ be-came o - be - di-ent for us, o - be - di - ent for us, ev - en to death, dy-ing on a cross.

There - fore God raised him on high and gave him a name, a name above all oth-er names.

Third Setting

Anthony Milner

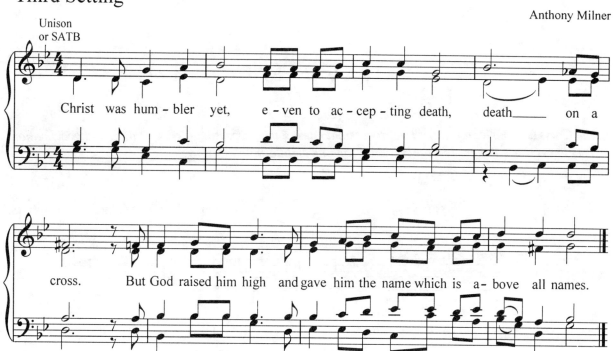

Unison or SATB

Christ was hum-bler yet, e-ven to ac-cep-ting death, death____ on a cross. But God raised him high and gave him the name which is a-bove all names.

Other settings will be found on pages 19 - 20

THE GENERAL INTERCESSIONS

The Intercessions may be sung in whole or in part. A simple tone is to be found in the Altar Missal. A suggested method is:

Deacon or Cantor I sings the first part of the prayer which announces the intention.

Cantor II leads a congregational response, for example:

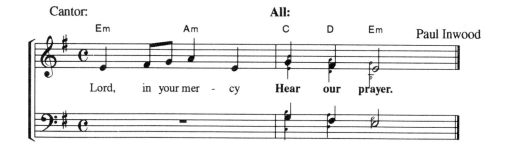

Cantor: **All:** Paul Inwood

Lord, in your mer - cy **Hear our prayer.**

PART TWO: THE VENERATION OF THE CROSS

The Cross is brought into church in procession. During the procession there is a threefold acclamation, as below. Overleaf there is a processional song as an alternative.

First Setting

Dom Gregory Murray, O.S.B.

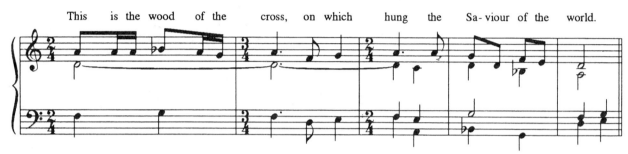

This is the wood of the cross, on which hung the Sa- viour of the world.

ALL:

Come, let us wor - ship.

Second Setting

Paschal Jordan, O.P.

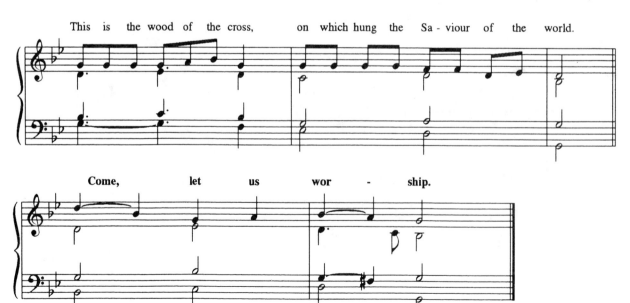

This is the wood of the cross, on which hung the Sa - viour of the world.

Come, let us wor - ship.

For information on copyright, see acknowledgements page

Third Setting

Pachal Jordan

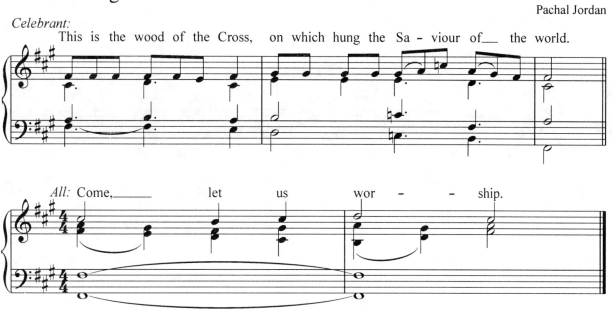

Celebrant:
This is the wood of the Cross, on which hung the Sa - viour of__ the world.

All: Come,_____ let us wor - - ship.

Fourth Setting

This is sung three times. The pitch is raised for each repetition.

Source not traced

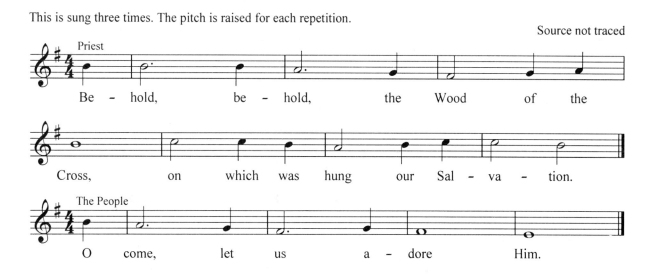

Priest
Be - hold, be - hold, the Wood of the

Cross, on which was hung our Sal - va - tion.

The People
O come, let us a - dore Him.

Processional song of the Cross

Paul Inwood

This song may be used in the procession of the Cross. It is sung continously and not three times as with
This is wood of the Cross (previous page). It is similar to the former, however, in having parts for the
priest to sing, in dialogue with cantor and All.

Cantor:

ALL REPEAT *refrain from 'Come, come, let us adore.' Then the whole of the previous page is repeated, i.e. first the priest then All sing the whole refrain. Verse 2 follows:*

Text: Harold Winstone

The procedure following verse 1 is repeated. **ALL REPEAT** *refrain from 'Come, come, let us adore.' Then the whole of the previous page is repeated, i.e. first the priest then All sing the whole refrain. to conclude the song.*

Music and Hymns during the Veneration

THE REPROACHES

First Setting

Plainchant, adapted by
David Kingsley

ANTIPHON I

My peo - ple, what have I done to you? How have I of-fen - ded you? Ans - wer me.

ANTIPHON II

Ho - ly is God! Ho - ly and strong! Ho - ly im - mor - tal One, have mer - cy on us!

Chant Formulae A-D:

The distribution of the text among groups of singers may be done as in the Missal; or a cantor may sing the chanted verses, the choir singing the Antiphons; or any other suitable distribution may be used.
Letters at the beginning of each line of text refer to the music above.

I	My people...
A	I led you out of Egypt, from slavery to /free/dom,
B	but you led your Saviour / to the / cross.
I	My people...
II	Holy is God...
A	For forty years I led you safely through the /de/sert.
A	I fed you with manna from /hea/ven,
A	and brought you to a land of /plen/ty;
B	but you led your Saviour / to the / cross.
II	Holy is God...

For information on copyright, see acknowledgements page

A	What more could I have /done/ for you?
A	I planted you as my fairest vine,
B	but you yielded / only / bitterness:
A	when I was thirsty you gave me vinegar to drink,
B	and you pierced your Saviour / with a / lance.
II	Holy is God..

C	For your sake I scourged your captors and first/born/ sons,
D	but you brought your scourges / down on / me.
I	My people...

A	I led you from slavery to /free/dom
B	and drowned your captors / in the / sea,
D	but you handed me over / to your / high priests.
I	My people...

C	I opened the sea /be/fore you,
D	but you opened my side / with a / spear.
I	My people...

A	I led you on your way in a pillar /of/ cloud,
B	but you led me to / Pilate's / court.
I	My people...

C	I bore you up with manna in /the/ desert,
D	but you struck me / down and / scourged me.
I	My people...

A	I gave you saving water from /the/ rock,
B	but you gave me gall and vine/gar to / drink.
I	My people...

C	For you I struck down the kings /of/ Canaan,
D	but you struck my head / with a / reed.
I	My people...

A	I gave you a royal /scep/tre,
B	but you gave me a / crown of / thorns.
I	My people...

C	I raised you to the height /of/ majesty,
D	but you have raised me high / on a / cross.
I	My people...

Second Setting

Kevin Mayhew

RESPONSE 1

My peo - ple, what have I done to you?

How have I of - fen - ded you? An - swer me.

Verse

I led you out of Egypt, from slave - ry to freedom, but you led your Sa - viour to the cross.

RESPONSE 2

Ha - gi-os o The - os. Ho-ly is God. Ha - gi-os i - schy - ros,

Ho-ly and strong. Ha - gi - os a - tha - na - tos, e - le - i - son

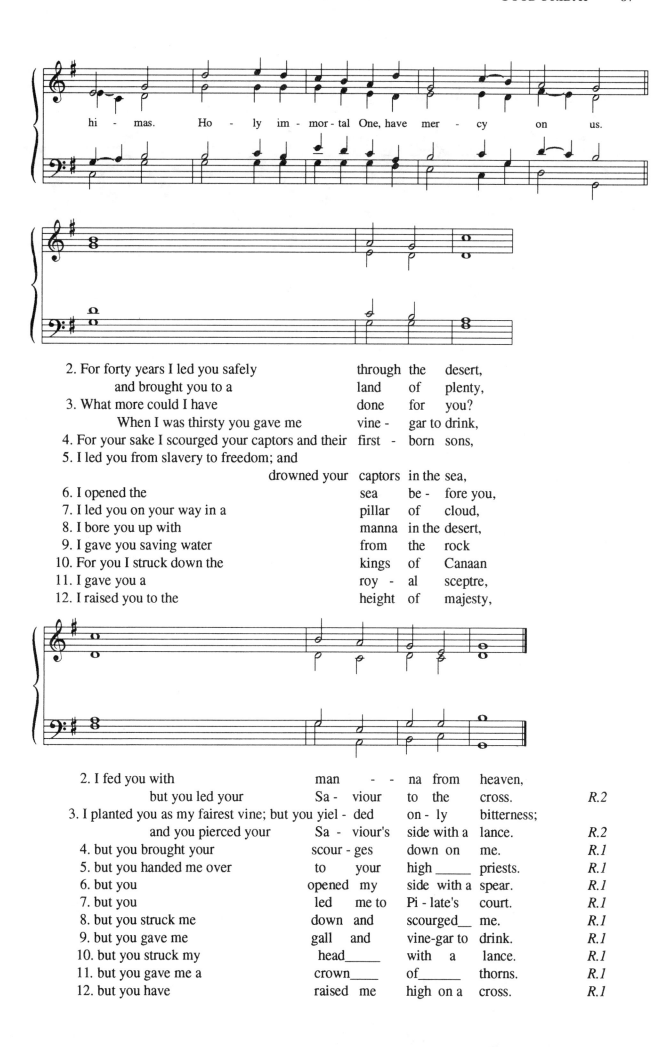

hi - mas.   Ho - ly im - mor-tal One, have mer - cy   on   us.

2. For forty years I led you safely   through the   desert,
        and brought you to a   land   of   plenty,
3. What more could I have   done   for   you?
        When I was thirsty you gave me   vine - gar to drink,
4. For your sake I scourged your captors and their first - born sons,
5. I led you from slavery to freedom; and
                        drowned your captors in the sea,
6. I opened the   sea   be - fore you,
7. I led you on your way in a   pillar   of   cloud,
8. I bore you up with   manna   in the desert,
9. I gave you saving water   from   the   rock
10. For you I struck down the   kings   of   Canaan
11. I gave you a   roy -   al   sceptre,
12. I raised you to the   height of   majesty,

2. I fed you with   man - - na from   heaven,
        but you led your   Sa - viour   to the   cross.   R.2
3. I planted you as my fairest vine; but you yiel - ded   on - ly   bitterness;
        and you pierced your   Sa - viour's side with a lance.   R.2
4. but you brought your   scour - ges   down on   me.   R.1
5. but you handed me over   to   your   high ____ priests.   R.1
6. but you   opened my   side with a spear.   R.1
7. but you   led   me to Pi - late's court.   R.1
8. but you struck me   down   and   scourged__ me.   R.1
9. but you gave me   gall   and   vine-gar to drink.   R.1
10. but you struck my   head_____   with a   lance.   R.1
11. but you gave me a   crown____   of_____ thorns.   R.1
12. but you have   raised me   high on a cross.   R.1

Third Setting

Peter Jones

Fourth Setting

Anthony Milner

For information on copyright, see acknowledgements page

mor - tal One, have mer - cy on us.

For for - ty years I led you safe - ly through the de - sert. I fed you with man - na from

Repeat 'Holy is God'

hea - ven, and brought you to a land of plen - ty, but you led your Sa - viour to the Cross.

What more could I have done for you? I plan - ted you as my fai - rest vine, but you yiel - ded

on - ly bit - ter - ness:__ When I was thir - sty you gave me vi - ne - gar to

drink and you pierced your Sa - viour with a lance.

Repeat 'Holy is God'

ending A

1.For your sake I scourged your   captors, and their   first - born   sons,
2.I led you from slavery   to   freedom, and drowned your captors in the   sea,
3.I opened the (to ending B)
4.I led you on   your   way in a   pillar   of   cloud,
5.I bore you up with (to ending B)
6.I gave you saving   water from the   rock,
7.For you I struck down the   (to ending B)
8.I gave you a (to ending B)
9.I raised you to the (to ending B)

For information on copyright, see acknowledgements page

ending B

Repeat 'O, my people' after each verse.

1._	but you have brought your	scour-ges down on me.
2._	but you handed me over	to your high___ priests.
3.sea be - fore you,	but you opened my	side___ with a spear.
4._	but you led me to	Pi - late's___ court.
5.manna in the de - sert,	but you struck me	down and scourged_ me.
6._	but you gave me gall and	vi - ne - gar to drink.
7.kings of Ca - naan,	but you struck my	head___ with a reed.
8.Roy - al scep - tre,	but you gave me a	crown___ of___ thorns.
9.height of ma - jesty,	but you have raised me	high___ on a Cross.

Fifth Setting

Paschal Jordan

Refrain: My peo-ple, what have I done to you? How have I of-fen-ded you? An-swer me!

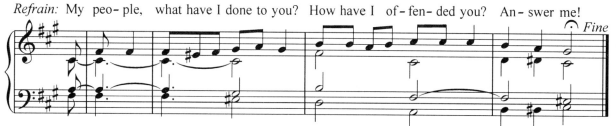

Fine

Verses: two equal voices and instrumental bass

D.C.

1. I led you out of Egypt,
   from slave<u>ry</u> to freedom;
   but you led your Saviour <u>to</u> the Cross.

2. I led you from slavery to freedom
   and drowned your captors <u>in</u> the sea;
   but you handed me over to <u>your</u> high priests.

3. I opened the <u>sea</u> before you,
   but you opened my side <u>with</u> a spear.

4. I led you on your way in a pi<u>llar</u> of cloud,
   but you led me to <u>Pi</u>late's court.

5. I bore you up with manna <u>in</u> the desert,
   but you struck me <u>down</u> and scourged me.

6. I gave you saving water <u>from</u> the rock,
   but you gave me gall and vine<u>gar</u> to drink.

7. For you I struck down the <u>kings</u> of Canaan,
   but you struck my head <u>with</u> a reed.

8. I gave you a <u>royal</u> sceptre,
   but you gave me a <u>crown</u> of thorns.

9. I raised you to the <u>height</u> of majesty,
   but you have raised me high <u>on</u> a cross.

Sixth Setting

Chris O'Hara

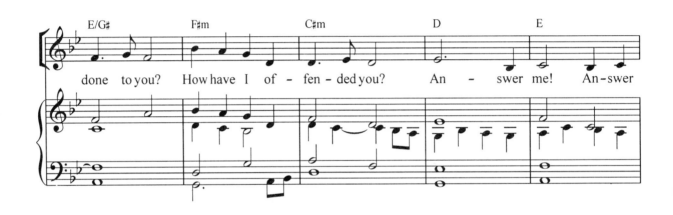

For information on copyright, see acknowledgements page

Verses   Cantor

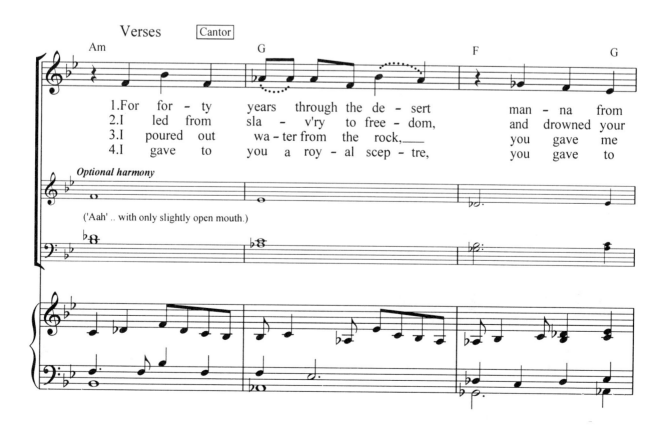

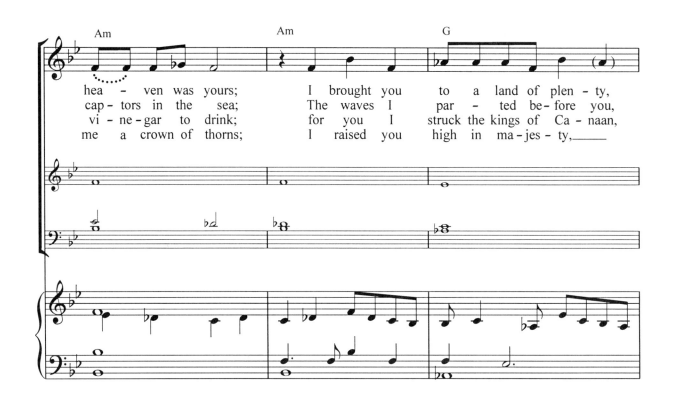

hea - ven was yours;   I brought you   to a land of plen - ty,
cap - tors in the sea;   The waves I   par - ted be - fore you,
vi - ne - gar to drink;   for you I   struck the kings of Ca - naan,
me a crown of thorns;   I raised you   high in ma - jes - ty,____

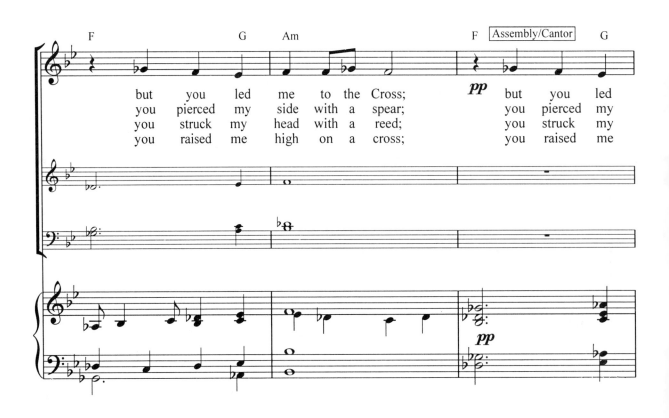

but you led me to the Cross;   but you led
you pierced my side with a spear;   you pierced my
you struck my head with a reed;   you struck my
you raised me high on a cross;   you raised me

Assembly/Cantor

For information on copyright, see acknowledgements page

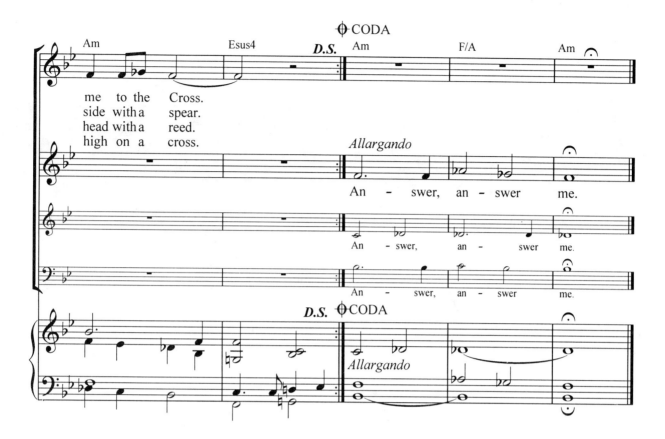

Seventh Setting

Words (based on the Reproaches)
and Music: Damian Lundy

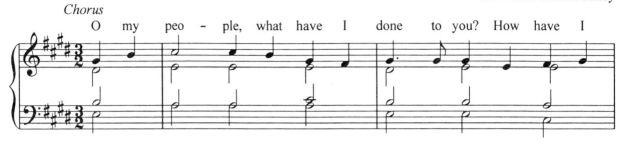

Chorus

O my peo - ple, what have I done to you? How have I

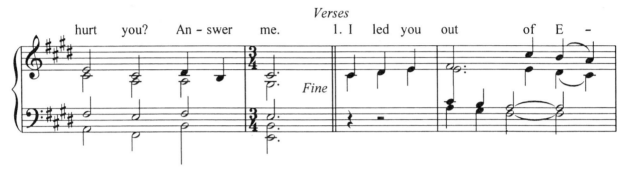

hurt you? An - swer me. *Verses* 1. I led you out of E -

Fine

- gypt, From sla - ve - ry I set you free. I brought you

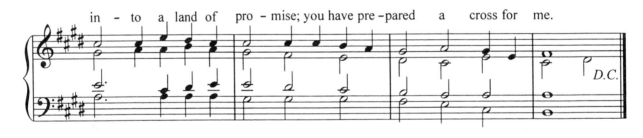

in - to a land of pro - mise; you have pre -pared a cross for me.

D.C.

2 I led you as a shepherd,
   I brought you safely through the sea,
   fed you with manna in the desert;
   you have prepared a cross for me.
       Chorus

3 I fought for you in battles,
   I won you strength and victory,
   gave you a royal crown and sceptre:
   you have prepeared a cross for me.
       Chorus

4 I planted you, my vineyard;
   and cared for you most tenderly,
   looked for abundant fruit, and found none
   - only the cross you made for me.
       Chorus

5 Then listen to my pleading,
   and do not turn away from me.
   You are my people: will you reject me?
   For you I suffer bitterly.
       Chorus

The Trisagion

The Trisagion, or parts of it, could be sung in conjunction with Damian Lundy's Reproaches.
The alternating Greek and Latin are traditionally sung by Choir 1 and Choir 2.
A solo voice or semi-chorus (Choir 1) might make an effective contrast to the main body of singers (Choir 2).

* The sign ♫ does not represent an ornament but a 'quilisma',
a note sung lightly, the note before being slightly lengthened.
(The melody is just as beautiful if you ignore the quilismas.)

Eighth Setting

Finlandia
10 10 10 10 10 10

Music: Jean Sibelius (1865-1957)
Text: Michael Forster, based on the Reproaches

1. I give you love, and how do you re-pay?_____ When you were slaves I strove to set you free;_____ I led you out from un-der Pha-roh's yoke,_____ but you led out your Christ to Cal-va-ry._____ My peo-ple, tell me, what is my of-fence?_____ What have I done to harm you? Ans-wer me!

2 For forty years I was your constant guide,
  I fed you with my manna from on high.
  I led you out to live in hope and peace,
  but you led out my only Son to die.

3 With cloud and fire I marked the desert way,
  I heard your cries of rage and calmed your fear.
  I opened up the sea and led you through,
  but you have opened Christ with nail and spear.

4 When in distress you cried to me for food,
  I sent you quails in answer to your call,
  and saving water from the desert rock,
  but to my Son you offered bitter gall.

5 I gave you joy when you were in despair,
  with songs of hope, I set your hearts on fire;
  crowned you with grace, the people of my choice,
  but you have crowned my Christ with thorny briar.

6 When you were weak, exploited and oppressed,
  I heard your cry and listened to your plea.
  I raised you up to honour and renown,
  but you have raised me on a shameful tree.

Ninth Setting

Words, based on the Reproaches,
and Music: Francesca Leftly

Melody
Harmony I / II

Chorus — Dm — Am

My peo - ple, what have I done to you?____

Ah*

Gm7 — Am — Dm — *Fine*

—— How have I hurt you? An - swer me.

Ah

Verse — Dm — Bb — C — Am — Dm — Gm

1. I led you____ out of E - gypt,____ I set you free;____ I set you

Dm — Bb — C

free.____ I led you____ through the de - sert____

Am — Dm — Gm — Dm — *D.C.*

—— and yet you turn____ a - way from me.

* or instruments

2 I fed you in the desert,
   I led you through the raging sea.
   I gave you saving water
   and yet you found a cross for me.

3 I gave you a royal sceptre;
   you offered me a crown of thorns.
   I raised you as a nation;
   you mocked and treated me with scorn.

Tenth Setting

John Rombaut

Écrit au bas d'un Crucifix

Words: Victor Hugo
Music: Estelle White

For information on copyright, see acknowledgements page

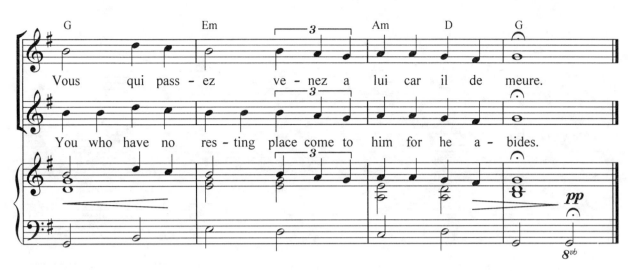

Vous qui pass - ez ve - nez a lui car il de meure.

You who have no res - ting place come to him for he a - bides.

My Lord, my master

Leinthall Starkes (11 10 11 10)   Paul Davis

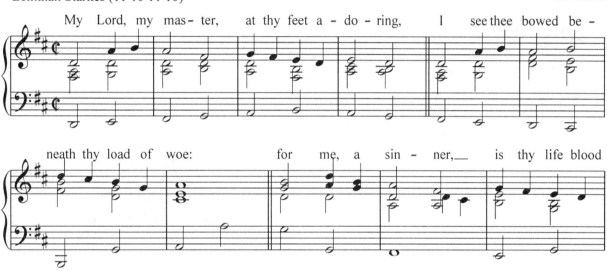

My Lord, my mas - ter, at thy feet a - do - ring, I see thee bowed be -

neath thy load of woe: for me, a sin - ner,___ is thy life blood

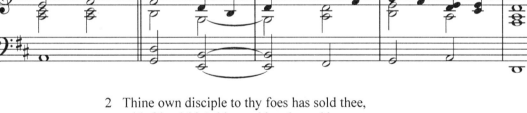

pour - ing; for thee, my Sa - viour scarce my tears will flow.

2 Thine own disciple to thy foes has sold thee,
 with friendship's kiss and loyal word he came:
 how oft of faithful love my lips have told thee,
 while thou hast seen my falsehood and my shame!

3 With taunts amd scoffs they mock what seems thy weakness,
 with blows and outrage adding pain to pain;
 thou art unmoved and steadfast in thy meekness:
 when I am wronged how quickly I complain!

4 O victim of thy love, O pangs most healing,
 O saving death, O wounds that I adore,
 O shame most glorious! Christ, before thee kneeling,
 I pray thee keep me thine for evermore.

Jaques Bridaine 1701-1767
tr. Thomas Benson Pollock 1836-1896

Vexilla Regis

Gonfalon Royal (LM)

Percy Buck 1871-1947

The roy-al ban-ners forward go, the cross shines forth in my-stic glow; where he in flesh, our flesh who made, our sen-tence bore, our ran-som paid.

2 There whilst he hung, his sacred side
by soldier's spear was opened wide,
to cleanse us in the precious flood
of water mingled with his blood.

3 Fulfilled is now what David told
in true prophetic song of old,
how God the heathen's king should be;
for God is reigning from the tree.

4 O tree of glory, tree most fair,
ordained those holy limbs to bear,
how bright in purple robe it stood,
the purple of a Saviour's blood!

Optional Amen. A - men

5 Upon its arms, like balance true,
he weighed the price for sinners due,
the price which none but he could pay:
and spoiled the spoiler of his prey.

6 To thee, eternal Three in One,
let homage meet by all be done,
as by the cross thou dost restore,
so rule and guide us evermore. (Amen.)

Venantius Fortunatus (530-609)
tr. J.M.Neale (1818-1866), alt.

Second Tune

Eisenach (LM)

J H Schein. Harmony: J S Bach

For information on copyright, see acknowledgements page

Original Version

The roy - al ban - ners for - ward go, the cross shines forth in my - stic glow,
Ve-xil - la re - gis pro - de unt, ful- get Cru-cis my- ste - ri - um,

where he in flesh, our flesh who made, our sen - tence bore, our ran - som paid.
qua vi- ta, mor - tem per - tu- lit, et mor - te vi - tam pro - tu- lit.

A - men.

2. Quae vulnerata lanceae
mucrone diro, criminum
ut nos lavaret sordibus,
manavit unda et sanguine.

3. Impleta sunt, quae concinit
David fideli carmine,
dicendo nationibus:
regnavit a ligno Deus.

4. Arbor decora et fulgida,
ornata Regis purpura
electa digno stipite
tam sancta membra tangere.

5. Beata, cujus brachiis
pretium pependit saeculi,
statera facta corporis,
tulitque praedam tartari.

6. O crux, ave, spes unica
hoc Passionis tempore
piis adauge gratiam
reisque dele crimina.

7. Te, fons salutis Trinitas
collaudet omnis spiritus;
quibus crucis victoriam
largiris, adde praemium. Amen.

Venantius Fortunatus (530-609) alt.

* *English translation of this verse:*

O Cross, our one reliance, Hail!
So may this Passiontide avail
To give fresh merit to the saint
And pardon to the penitent.
Tr. J. M. Neale

Adoramus te, Christe

Attrib. Palestrina 1524-1594

For information on copyright, see acknowledgements page

O vos omnes

Giovanni Croce 1557-1609

* For a shorter motet finish here, omitting bars 22-29 and the repeat.

Ave verum

W. A. Mozart
1756-1791

For information on copyright, see acknowledgements page

Pie Jesu
(from the Requiem)

Gabriel Faure 1845-1924

From the full score of 1910.
This version copyright 2001 by McCrimmon Publishing Co. Ltd.

For information on copyright, see acknowledgements page

Do - mi - ne,   do - na_ e - is,   do - na e - is   sem - pi - ter - nam

re - qui - em,   sem - pi - ter - nam   re - qui - em.

(Ped. *pp*)

Drop, drop, slow tears

Song 46 (10 10)

First strain of Song 46
Orlando Gibbons 1583-1625

1. Drop, drop, slow tears,
     And bathe those beauteous feet,
   Which brought from heaven
     The news and Prince of peace.

2. Cease not, wet eyes,
     His mercies to entreat;
   To cry for vengeance
     Sin doth never cease.

3. In your deep floods
     Drown all my faults and fears;
   Nor let his eye
     See sin, but through my tears.

Phineas Fletcher 1582-1650

Pie Jesu

1st time: soloist and organ
2nd time: choir only
3rd time: solo and choir

John Rombaut

1st & 2nd times | Last time

-pe – tu – a   lu – ce – at   e – is.   e – is.

Now my soul

Santeuil 878787   Paul Davis

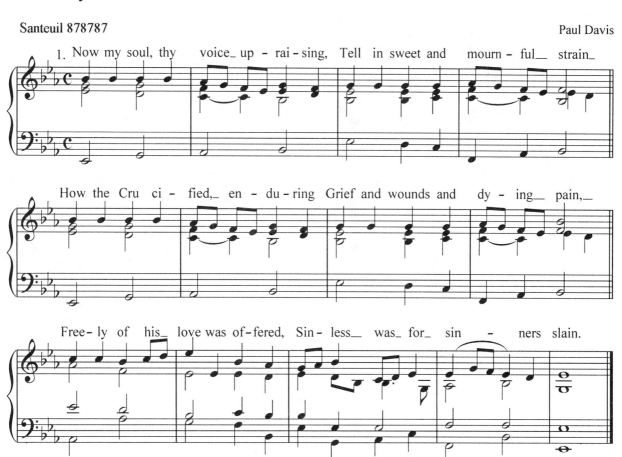

1. Now my soul, thy voice_ up – rai – sing, Tell in sweet and mourn – ful_ strain_
How the Cru ci – fied,_ en – du – ring Grief and wounds and dy – ing_ pain,_
Free – ly of his_ love was of-fered, Sin – less_ was_ for_ sin – ners slain.

2. See, his hands and feet are fastened!
   So he makes his people free;
   Not a wound whence Blood is flowing
   But a fount of grace shall be;
   Yea, the very nails which nail him
   Nail us also to the Tree.

3. Jesu, may those precious fountains
   Drink to thirsty souls afford;
   Let them be our cup and healing,
   And at length our full reward:
   So a ransomed world shall ever
   Praise thee, its redeeming Lord.

Claude de Santeuil 1628-84
Tr. H W Baker 1821-77

God so loved the world

Quartet or Chorus (unaccompanied) from 'The Crucifixion'

Sir John Stainer
1840-1901

For information on copyright, see acknowledgements page

For information on copyright, see acknowledgements page

Crucem tuam

Ostinato Chorale

Jaques Berthier (1923-1994)

The upper voice is sung one or more times in unison, then the second voice is added and finally the choir

What Wondrous Love

This song is effective when sung unaccompanied.
WONDROUS LOVE

From 'Southern Harmony', 1835
Arranged by Stephen Dean

2. When I was sinking down, sinking down,
       sinking down,
   when I was sinking down, sinking down;
   When I was sinking down
   beneath God's righteous frown,
   Christ laid aside his crown for my soul, for
       my soul,
   Christ laid aside his crown for my soul.

3. To God and to the Lamb I will sing, I will sing
   To God and to the Lamb I will sing, I will sing;
   To God and to the Lamb
   who is the great I AM,
   while millions join the theme, I will sing, I will sing,
   while millions join the theme, I will sing.

4. And when from death I'm free, I'll sing on, I'll sing on
   And when from death I'm free, I'll sing on, I'll sing on
   And when from death I'm free
   I'll sing on and joyful be,
   and through eternity I'll sing on, I'll sing on,
   and through eternity I'll sing on.

Rev. Alexander Means (1801-1853)

Veronica's Litany

Joanne Boyce
arr. Chris Rolinson

D.S. for verses.
Coda after v 4.   **CODA**

Bleeding hands,_____
spoken pain,_____
bandoned Lord,_____
Stumbling Lord,_____

What have they done?   What have they

done to you   Lord?_____   What have they

done to you___ Lord?_____

Jesus, remember me

Jaques Berthier (1923-1994)

Jesus, remember me when you come into your Kingdom.

Jesus, remember me when you come into your Kingdom.

When I survey

Music: Roger Jones
Text: Isaac Watts (1674-1748)

Andante cantabile con espressione

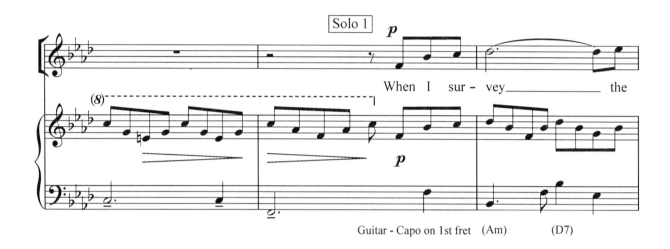

Solo 1

When I sur-vey_____ the

Guitar - Capo on 1st fret   (Am)   (D7)

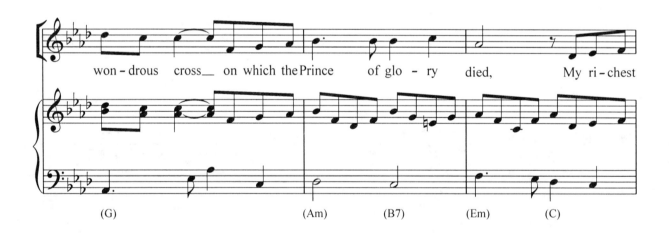

won-drous cross__ on which the Prince of glo-ry died, My ri-chest

(G)   (Am)   (B7)   (Em)   (C)

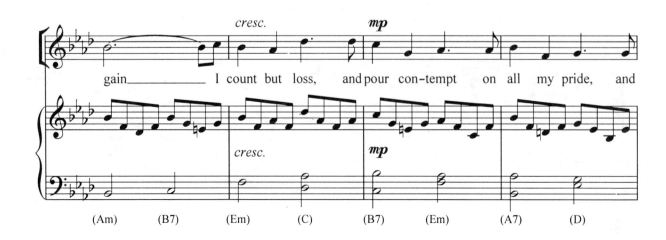

gain_____ I count but loss, and pour con-tempt on all my pride, and

cresc.   mp

(Am)   (B7)   (Em)   (C)   (B7)   (Em)   (A7)   (D)

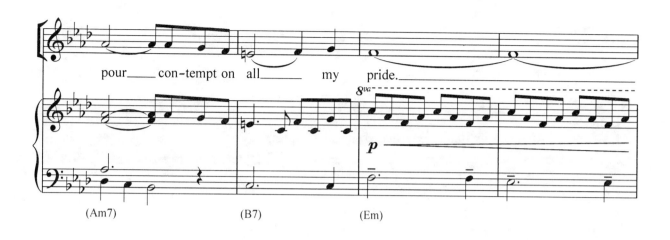

pour___con-tempt on all___ my pride.___

(Am7)   (B7)   (Em)

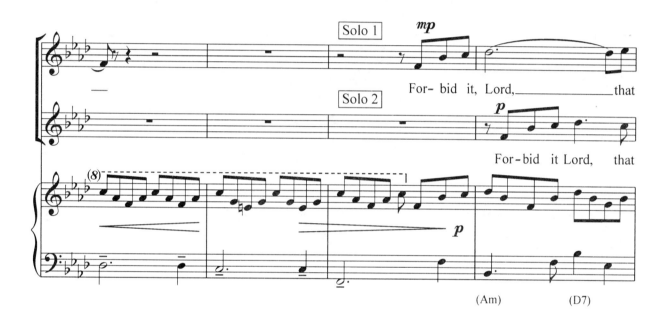

Solo 1   *mp*

For- bid it, Lord,_____that

Solo 2

For-bid it Lord,   that

(Am)   (D7)

I should   boast,_ save in the death   of Christ my   God;   All the vain

I should   boast_   Save in the   death   of Christ my   God;__

(G)   (Am)   (B7)   (Em)   (C)

things_____ that charm me most,   I   sac - ri - fice   them

All the vain things   that charm me   most;   I   sac - ri - fice   them

(Am)   (B7)   (Em)   (C)   (B7)   (Em)

to   his   blood,   I   sac - ri-fice them to_____ his   blood._____

to   his   blood,   I   sac - ri-fice them to   his   blood._____

(A7)   (D)   (Am7)   (B7)   (Em)

See from his

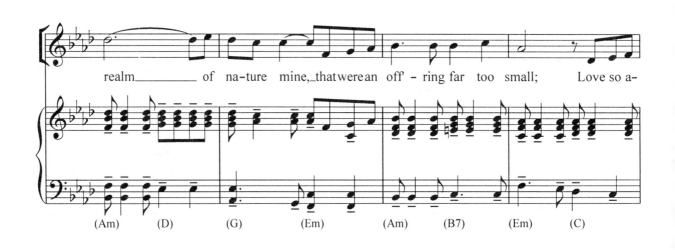

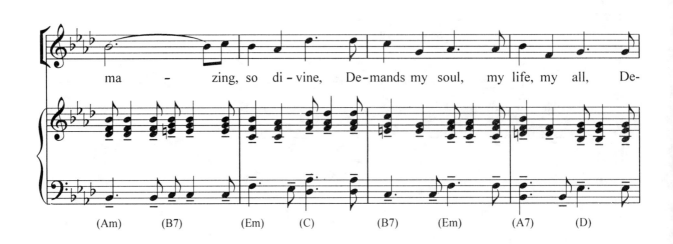

For information on copyright, see acknowledgements page

mands___ my soul, my   life,_____ my   all!_____

De

(C)   (Am7)   (B7)   (Em)   (Em7)

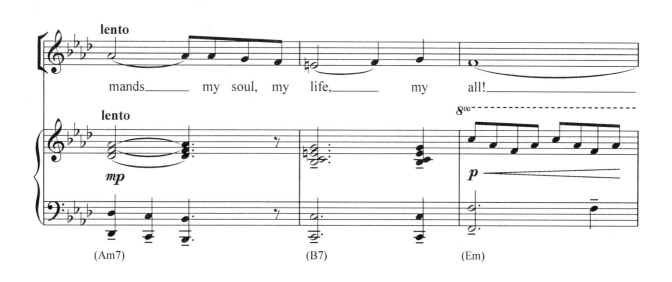

mands_____ my soul, my   life,_____ my   all!_____

(Am7)   (B7)   (Em)

The Easter Vigil
PART ONE: THE SERVICE OF LIGHT

This is sung three times: (1) at the beginning of the procession (2) at the church door (3) before the altar. The pitch is raised for each repetition. The deacon (or priest) sings alone, and the people respond.

First Setting

Christ our light.
or The light of Christ.
or Christ is our light.

The Missal

Thanks be to God.

(Latin)

Lu – men Chris – ti.

De – o gra – ti – as.

Second Setting

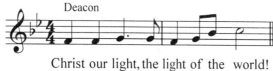

Christ our light, the light of the world!

Garfield Rochard

Let us give thanks to the Lord our God!

Third Setting

Christ our___ light!

Thanks be to God!

Fourth Setting

Light_ of___ Christ.___

Paschal Jordan

Thanks_ be to God.

For information on copyright, see acknowledgements page

The Exsultet - First Setting

The Ancient Plainsong for the Easter Proclamation (The Exsultet)
This should be sung by a Deacon or Priest
but may be sung by a lay Cantor 'if necessary'.

For information on copyright, see acknowledgements page

How bound - less your mer - ci - ful love! To ran - som a slave you gave a - way_ your Son.

O_____ hap - py fault, O ne - ces - sa - ry sin_ of A - dam, which gained for us so

great a Re - dee - mer! Most_ blessed_ of all nights, cho - sen by God to see Christ ri - sing

from the dead! Of this night scrip - ture says: "The night will be clear as day: it will be - come

my light,_ my joy." The power of this ho - ly night dis - pels_____ all_ e - vil,

wash - es guilt a - way, re - stores_ lost in - no - cence, brings_ mourn - ers joy;

it casts out hat - red, brings_ us peace, and hum - bles earth - ly pride.

Continue with either the Full Form or the Short Form.

Full Form

Night tru - ly blessed when hea - ven is wed - ded to earth and man is re - con - ciled with God. There - fore,

hea - ven - ly Fa - ther, in the joy_ of this_ night, re - ceive our eve - ning sac - ri - fice of praise,

your Chur - ch's so - lemn of - fer - ing. Ac - cept this Eas - ter can - dle,

a flame di - vi - ded but un - dimmed, a pil - lar of fire that glows to the ho - nour of God. Let it min - gle

with the lights_ of hea-ven and con-ti-nue brave-ly bur-ning to dis-pel the darkness of this night!

To Ending

Short Form

The power of this ho - ly night dis - pels___ all__ e - vil, wa-shes guilt a-way, re - stores_ lost in - no - cence and brings_ mour - ners joy. Ac - cept this Eas - ter can - dle. May it al - ways dis - pel the dark - ness of this night!

Ending for both Forms

May the Mor - ning Star which ne - ver sets find this flame_ still bur - ning: Christ__ that Mor - ning Star, who came back from the dead, and shed his peace - ful light_

People

on all__ man - kind, your Son who lives and reigns for e - ver and e - ver. A - men.

Second Setting

Dom Gregory Murray

This should be sung by a Deacon or Priest but may be sung by a lay Cantor 'if necessary',
in which case the bracketed section must be omitted.

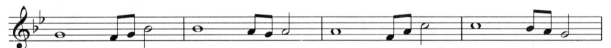

1 Rejoice, heavenly powers! Sing, <u>choirs</u> of angels!
   Exult, all creation <u>around</u> God's throne!
   Jesus Christ, our <u>King</u> is risen;
   Sound the trumpet <u>of</u> salvation!

2 Rejoice, O earth, in <u>shining</u> splendour,
   radiant in the brightness <u>of</u> your King!
   Christ has conquered! <u>Glory</u> fills you!
   Darkess vani<u>shes</u> for ever!

3 Rejoice, O Mother Church! <u>Exult</u> in glory!
   The risen Saviour <u>shines</u> upon you!
   Let this place re<u>sound</u> with joy,
   Echoing the mighty song of <u>all</u> God's people!

(4) (My dearest friends, standing with me in this <u>holy</u> light,
   join me in asking <u>God</u> for mercy,
   that he may give his un<u>worthy</u> minister
   grace to sing his <u>Easter</u> praises.)

See page 126 for optional congregational refrains.

chains of death and rose triumphant from the grave. **(*R.)** What good would life have been to us,

had Christ not come as our Redee - mer? Fa-ther, how wonder - ful your care for us!

How boundless your mer - ci - ful love! To ransom a slave you gave a-way your Son.

O happy fault, O necessary sin of Adam, which gained for us so great a Re-dee - mer! **(*R.)**

Most bles - sed of all nights, cho - sen by God to see Christ rising from the dead!

Of this night Scripture says: 'The night will be as clear as day: it will become my light, my joy.'

The power of this holy night dispels all evil, washes guilt a - way, re - stores lost innocence,

brings mour - ners joy; it casts out hatred, brings us peace, and hum - bles earth - ly pride.

Night truly blessed, when heaven is wed ded to earth and man is recon - ciled with God! **(*R.)**

There-fore, heavenly Father, in the joy of this night, re - ceive this evening sacri- fice of praise,

your Chur-ch's so - lemn of - fer - ing. Ac-cept this Easter candle , a flame divided but un-dimmed,

a pil lar of fire that glows to the hon-our of God. Let it mingle with the lights of hea-ven

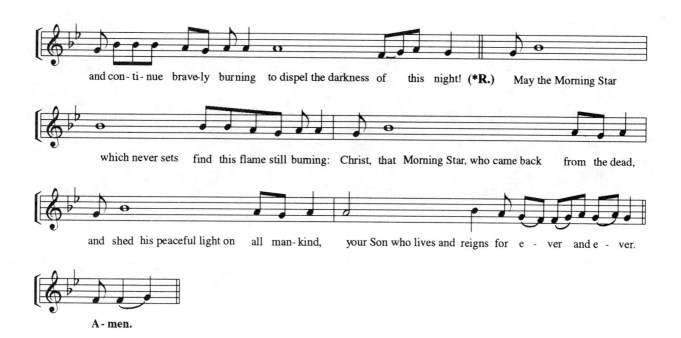

and con-ti-nue brave-ly burning to dispel the darkness of this night! (*R.) May the Morning Star

which never sets find this flame still burning: Christ, that Morning Star, who came back from the dead,

and shed his peaceful light on all man-kind, your Son who lives and reigns for e - ver and e - ver.

A - men.

OPTIONAL REFRAINS

Stephen Dean

One or more of the following refrains may be inserted at the points suggested (indicated by (*R.) in the text. They are intended to be sung by All but should be introduced and supported by Cantor or Choir

Refrain 1

Unaccompanied, or with support from a melody instrument (e.g. flute). Each phrase is sung first by or and repeated by All.

*This phrase should be varied as appropriate, e.g.:Rejoice to greet this holy night!
Rejoice to greet the death of sin!
Rejoice to greet the light of Christ!
Rejoice now in this Passover feast!

Refrain 2

A simple refrain which may be sung more frequently than indicated in the text. Keyboard accompaniment is suggested to allow transition back to the main text. May also be sung by SATB choir and All.

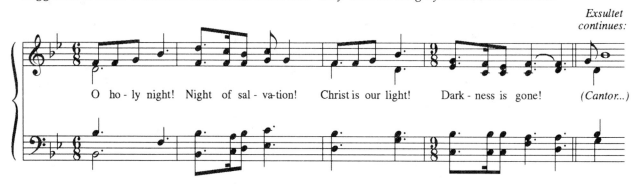

Refrain 3

Unaccompanied or with keyboard accompaniment.

Third Setting

Darwall's 148th
66 66 44 44

John Darwall (1731-1789)
arr. William Henry Monk (1823-1889)

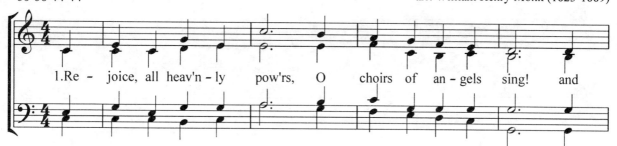

1.Re - joice, all heav'n - ly pow'rs, O choirs of an - gels sing! and

let the u - ni - verse with al - le - lu - ias ring! For Je - sus

lives in glo - ry bright, and end - less light to us he gives.

2. Rejoice, O shining earth,
in glorious hope reborn,
and praise the Light who wrought
the first creation's dawn.
Redeemed and free,
in Christ we rise,
and darkness dies
eternally.

3. Rejoice, O Mother church;
on you the Saviour shines:
then let the vaults resound
with joy and peace divine!
His truth proclaim,
and loud and long,
in glorious song,
exalt his name.

4. The people who have walked
in terror through the night,
from shades of death released,
have seen a glorious light.
God's word is sure,
and he will bless
with righteousness
the humble poor.

5. O God of hope and love,
who lit the desert way,
and led from slav'ry's night
to liberation's day:
still go before,
till we rejoice,
with heart and voice,
on Canaan's shore.

6. We light these gentle flames
to be our pledge and sign:
we share the risen life
of Christ, the light divine.
Throughout the earth,
oppression's night
shall flee the light
of human worth.

7. Arise, O Morning Star,
O Sun who never sets,
and bring these humble flames
to greater glory yet.
Let all adore,
in glorious strains,
the Christ who reigns
for evermore.

Michael Forster (b.1946)

Fourth Setting

Garfield Rochard

If the Exsultet is sang by a Cantor, the bracketed section must be omitted.
It is sung by a Deacon or Priest only.

For information on copyright, see acknowledgements page

All remaining verses

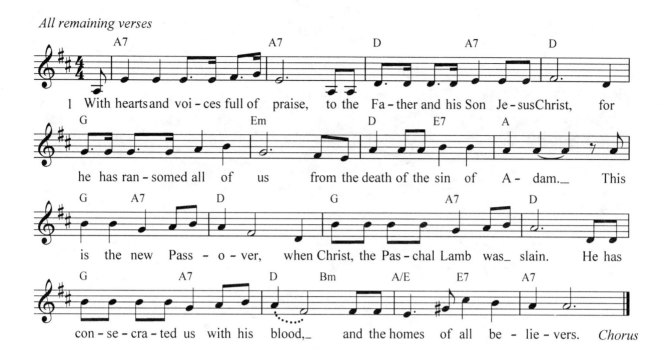

1 With hearts and voi - ces full of praise, to the Fa - ther and his Son Je - sus Christ, for
he has ran - somed all of us from the death of the sin of A - dam.__ This
is the new Pass - o - ver, when Christ, the Pas - chal Lamb was_ slain. He has
con - se - cra - ted us with his blood,_ and the homes of all be - lie - vers. *Chorus*

2 This is the night we remember,
  when Israel crossed the Red Sea.
  It's the night of the pillar of fire
  that destroyed the darkness of sin.
  It is the night of that washing,
  of a cleansing from all sin.
  It is the night of the grace of God
  When Christians grow in holiness.

3 This is the night of Resurrection,
  bursting the chains of death.
  The night of tremendous goodness,
  our Redeemer, the risen Jesus Christ.
  How wonderful your care for us, Father,
  how merciful and kind is your love.
  O happy fault of Adam,
  that gained so great a Redeemer.

4 God chose this night for us to see
  the rising of Jesus from the dead.
  This is the night of light and joy,
  this night has become clear as day.
  This is the night of love and true joy,
  of peace and the reign of goodness.
  This is the night when the heavens
  are wedded now to earth.

5 The joy of this night, Heavenly Father,
  is God reconciling us all.
  Receive now this Easter Candle,
  which glows to the honour of God.
  Let this light dispel all darkness.
  Let it meet Christ, the new Morning Star
  who came back from the dead triumphant
  and lives for ever and ever.

PART TWO: THE LITURGY OF THE WORD

RESPONSES WITHIN THE FIRST READING

First Setting

*The days may be marked by a sung response, changing the text at * as appropriate.*

Stephen Dean

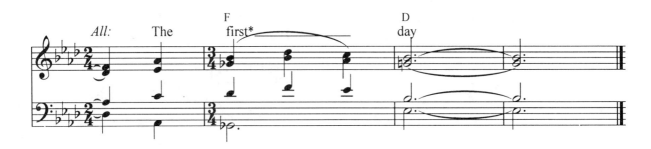

Second Setting

Christopher Walker

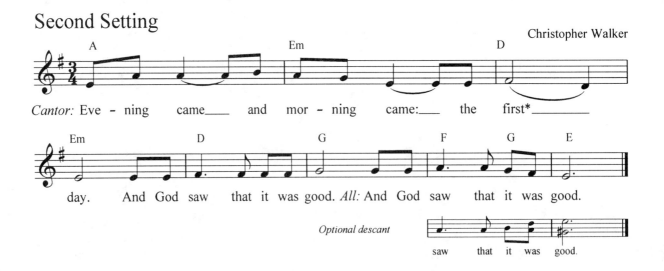

For information on copyright, see acknowledgements page

PSALM AFTER THE FIRST READING
First Setting

Dom Gregory Murray

Send forth your Spi-rit, O Lord,____ and re-new the face_ of the earth.

Sing the Psalm tone twice for each verse

1. Bless the <u>Lord</u>, my soul,
   Lord God, how <u>great</u> you are,
   clothed in majes<u>ty</u> and glory,
   wrapped in light as <u>in</u> a robe.

2. You founded the earth <u>on</u> its base,
   to stand firm from <u>age</u> to age.
   You wrapped it with the ocean <u>like</u> a cloak,
   the waters stood higher <u>than</u> the mountains.

3. You make springs gush forth <u>in</u> the valleys:
   they flow in be<u>tween</u> the hills.
   On their banks dwell the <u>birds</u> of heaven;
   from the branches they <u>sing</u> their song.

4. From your dwelling you wa<u>ter</u> the hills;
   earth drinks its fill <u>of</u> your gift.
   You make the grass grow <u>for</u> the cattle
   and the plants to <u>serve</u> man's needs.

5. How many are your <u>works</u>, O Lord!
   In wisdom you have <u>made</u> them all.
   The earth is full <u>of</u> your riches.
   Bless the <u>Lord</u>, my soul!

Second Setting

Paschal Jordan

Send forth your Spi-rit, O Lord, and re - new_ the_ face of the earth.

1. Bless the <u>Lord</u>, my <u>soul</u>,
   Lord God, how <u>great</u> you <u>are</u>,
   clothed in <u>majesty</u> and <u>glory</u>,
   wrapped in <u>light</u> as in a <u>robe</u>.

2. You founded the <u>earth</u> on its <u>base</u>,
   to stand firm from <u>age</u> to <u>age</u>.
   You wrapped it with the <u>ocean</u> like a <u>cloak</u>,
   the waters stood <u>higher</u> than the <u>mountains</u>.

3. You make springs gush <u>forth</u> in the <u>valleys</u>:
   they flow in be<u>tween</u> the <u>hills</u>.
   On their banks dwell the <u>birds</u> of <u>heaven</u>;
   from the branches they <u>sing</u> their <u>song</u>.

4. From your dwelling you <u>water</u> the <u>hills</u>;
   earth drinks its <u>fill</u> of your <u>gift</u>.
   You make the grass <u>grow</u> for <u>the</u> cattle
   and the plants to <u>serve</u> man's <u>needs</u>.

5. How many are your <u>works</u>, O <u>Lord</u>!
   In wisdom you have <u>made</u> them <u>all</u>.
   The earth is <u>full</u> of your <u>riches</u>.
   Bless the <u>Lord</u>, my <u>soul</u>!

Stephen Dean

Third Setting

Ps 104(103):1-2.5-6.10.12-14.24.25

INTRO *First Time only*

RESPONSE

Send forth your Spi - rit, O Lord,   and re - new   the face   of the   earth.

VERSES

1. Bless   the Lord,   my soul! Lord   God,   how   great   you   are.

Clothed   in   majesty   and   glory   wrapped   in light   as   in   a   robe.

2. You founded the earth on its base,
   to stand firm from age to age.
   You wrapped it with the ocean like a cloak,
   the waters stood higher than the mountains.

3. You make the springs gush forth in the valleys:
   they flow in between the hills.
   On their banks dwell the birds of heaven;
   from the branches they sing their song.

4. From your dwelling you water the hills;
earth drinks its fill of your gift.
You make the grass to grow for the cattle
and the plants to serve man's needs.

5. How many are your works, O Lord!
In wisdom you have made them all.
The earth is full of your riches.
Bless the Lord, my soul!

Verse 5: Alternative setting

With intensity

How ma-ny are your works, O Lord! In wis-dom you have made them all.

The earth is full of your ri-ches. Bless the Lord,

bless the Lord, my soul, my soul!

ALTERNATIVE PSALM AFTER THE FIRST READING

Anne Ward

First Setting

Psalm 32: 4-7, 12-13, 20, 22 R v.5

For information on copyright, see acknowledgements page

Second Setting

Response: Paul Davis
Verse: from A. Drese 1620-1701

The Lord fills the earth with his love.

Response

Verses

S/A

1. The word of the Lord is faithful and all his works to be trusted.
2. By his word the heavens were made, by the breath of his mouth all the stars.
3. They are happy, whose God is the Lord, the people he has chosen as his own.
4. Our soul is waiting for the Lord. The Lord is our help and our shield.

S/A/+T

1. The Lord loves justice and right and fills the earth with his love.
2. He col- lects the waves of the ocean; he stores up the depths of the sea.
3. From the heavens the Lord looks forth, he sees all the children of men.
4. May your love be u - - pon us, O Lord, as we place all our hope in you.

Verse can also be performed Ten/Bar/Bass.

PSALM AFTER THE SECOND READING
First Setting

Psalm 15: 5, 8-11 R v.1

John Glynn

Pre - serve me, God, I take re - fuge in you.

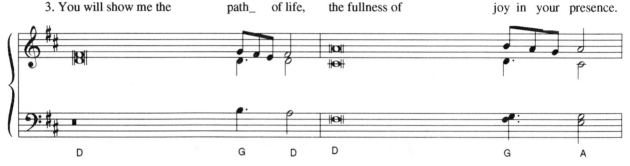

1. O Lord, it is you who are my por-tion and cup; it is you yourself who are_ my prize.
2. And so my heart rejoices, my soul _ is glad; even my body shall rest_ in safety.
3. You will show me the path_ of life, the fullness of joy in your presence.

1. I keep the Lord ever in my sight: since he is at my right hand, I shall stand firm.
2. For you will not leave my soul a-mong the dead nor let your beloved know de - cay.
3. (line omitted) at your right hand happiness for ever.

For information on copyright, see acknowledgements page

Second Setting

Paul Inwood

Third Setting

Christopher Walker
Words based on Psalm 15

For information on copyright, see acknowledgements page

Fourth Setting

Dom Gregory Murray

Pre - serve__ me,__ God, I take re - fuge in you.

Sing the Psalm tone twice for vv 1 & 2

1. O Lord, it is you who are my por<u>tion</u> and cup;
   it is you yourself who <u>are</u> my prize.
   I keep the Lord ever <u>in</u> my sight:
   since he is at my right hand, I <u>shall</u> stand firm.

2. And so my heart is rejoices, my <u>soul</u> is glad;
   even my body shall <u>rest</u> in safety.
   For you will not leave my soul a<u>mong</u> the dead,
   nor let your beloved <u>know</u> decay.

3. You will show me the path of life,
   the fullness of joy <u>in</u> your presence,
   at your right hand happi<u>ness</u> for ever.

Fifth Setting

Paschal Jordan

Pre - serve__ me,__ God, I take re - fuge in you.

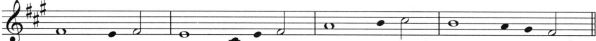

1. O Lord, it is you who are my portion <u>and</u> cup;
   it is you yourself who <u>are</u> my prize.
   I keep the Lord ever in <u>my</u> sight:
   since he is at my right hand, I <u>shall</u> stand firm.

2. And so my heart is rejoices, my soul <u>is</u> glad;
   even my body shall <u>rest</u> in safety.
   For you will not leave my soul among <u>the</u> dead,
   nor let your beloved <u>know</u> decay.

3. You will show me the path <u>of</u> life,
   the fullness of joy <u>in</u> your presence,   Omit 3rd quarter of tone
   at your right hand happi<u>ness</u> for ever.

For information on copyright, see acknowledgements page

THE THIRD READING (Exodus 15: 1-6, 17-18) finishes with the words:

It was then that Moses and the sons of Israel took up this song in honour of the Lord:

The choir takes up the Canticle immediately.

Canticle: First Setting

Exodus 15: 1-6, 17-18
Charmaine Abraham

I will sing to the Lord, glorious his tri-umph! Horse and ri-der he has thrown in-to the sea!

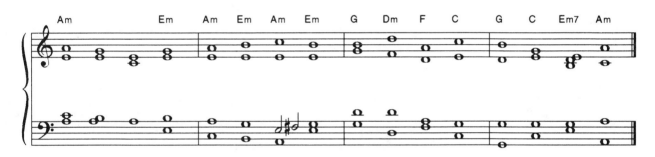

The Lord is my strength, my song, my salvation.
This is my God and I extol him.
My father's God and I give him praise,
the Lord is a warrior, the Lord is his name.

The chariots of Pharoah he hurled into the sea,
the flower of his army is drowned in the sea.   *(Omit C)*
The deeps hide them; they sank like a stone.

Your right hand, Lord, glorious in its power,
your right hand, Lord, has shattered the enemy.   *(Omit C)*
In the greatness of your glory you crushed the foe.

You will lead them and plant them on your mountain,
the place, O Lord, where you have made your home,
the sanctuary, Lord, which your hands have made,
the Lord will reign for ever and ever.

Second Setting

Stephen Dean

tol him; my fa - thers' God: I give him praise!

Verses 2-4:

2. The Lord is a war - ri - or! The Lord is his name. The
3. Your right hand, O__ Lord,__ full of power, Your
4. You will lead____ your peo - ple to your mountain, the

cha - riots of Pha - raoh he hurls in the sea. The flower of his
right hand is glo - rious in po - wer,_____ __ you crush____ your
place,___ O Lord, you have made__ your home; the sanc - tuary your

ar - my is drowned in the sea. The deeps____ hide them: they
foes in your strength, in great - ness of glo - ry you
hands have made. The Lord will reign for

sank like a stone.
shatt - ered the foe.
e - ver - more!

DESCANT TO RESPONSE (after vv3, 4)

I will sing to the Lord, glo - rious his tri - umph!

glo - rious his tri - umph! I will sing to the Lord.

Third Setting

Anthony Milner

Or this setting

Dom Gregory Murray

Omit 3rd quarter of tone in verse 3

1. I will sing to the Lord, glorious his triumph!
   Horse and rider he has thrown in<u>to</u> the sea!
   The Lord is my strength, my song, <u>my</u> salvation.
   This is my God and <u>I</u> extol him,
   my father's God and I <u>give</u> him praise.

2. The Lord is a warrior! The Lord <u>is</u> his name.
   The chariots of Pharaoh he hurled in<u>to</u> the sea,
   the flower of his army is drowned <u>in</u> the sea.
   The deeps hide them; they sank <u>like</u> a stone.

3. Your right hand, Lord, is glorious <u>in</u> its power,
   (*Your right hand, Lord, is glorious in its power,*)
   your right hand, Lord, has shat<u>tered</u> the enemy.
   In the greatness of your glory you <u>crushed</u> the foe.

(N.B. Different pointing for 4th Setting)

4. You will lead your people and plant them <u>on</u> your mountain,
   the place, O Lord, where you have <u>made</u> your home,
   the sanctuary, Lord, which your <u>hands</u> have made.
   The Lord will reign for e<u>ver</u> and ever.

Fourth Setting

Dom Gregory Murray

Sing the Psalm tone twice for vv 1, 2 & 4 Psalm text above. (N.B. v 3)

The FOURTH READING is taken from Isaiah 54: 5-14

PSALM AFTER THE FOURTH READING
First Setting

Psalm 29: 2, 4-6, 11-13 R v.2

Dom Gregory Murray

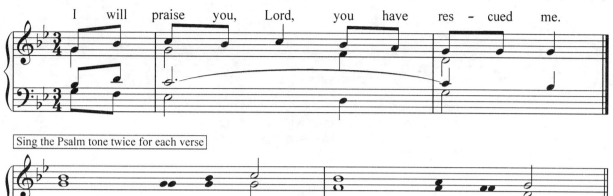

Sing the Psalm tone twice for each verse

Accents over syllables refer to Second setting.

1. I will praise you, Lord, you have rescued me
   and have not let my enemies rejoice over me.
   O Lord, you have raised my sóul from the dead,
   restored me to life from those who sink into the grave.

2. Sing psalms to the Lord, you who love him,
   give thanks to his holy name.
   His anger lasts but a moment; his fávour through life.
   At night there are tears, but joy comes with dawn.

3. The Lord listened and had pity.
   The Lord came to my help.
   For me you have changed my móurníng into dancing,
   O Lord my God, I will thank you for ever.

Second Setting

Text of Psalm as for previous setting. See also note below.

Fintan O'Carroll

Psalm text above.

Stephen Dean

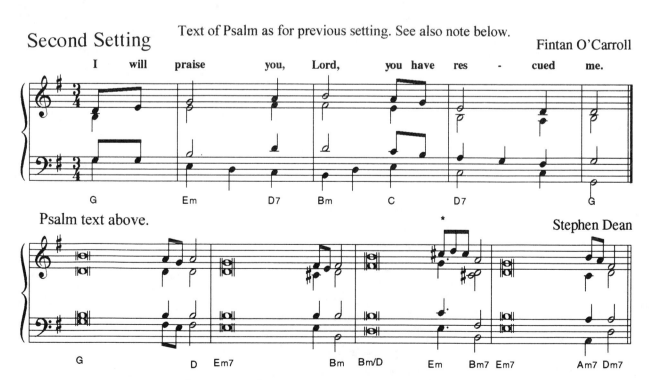

* In the 3rd quarter of this Psalm tone, change note on the accented syllable (sóul, fá-, móurning).
In v3 both syllables of *móurning* are sung on the c#.

Third Setting

Paschal Jordan

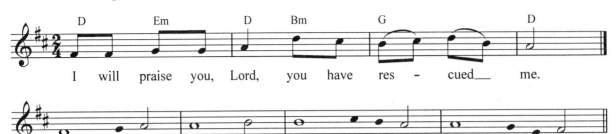

I will praise you, Lord, you have res - cued___ me.

1. I will praise you, Lord, you <u>have</u> rescued me
and have not let my enemies rejoice over <u>me</u>.
O Lord, you have raised my soul <u>from</u> the dead,
restored me to life from those who sink in<u>to</u> the grave.

2. Sing psalms to the Lord, you <u>who</u> love him,
give thanks to his holy <u>name</u>.
His anger lasts but a moment; his <u>fa</u>vour through life.
At night there are tears, but joy comes <u>with</u> the dawn.

3. The Lord listened and <u>had</u> pity.
The Lord came to my <u>help</u>.
For me you have changed my mourning <u>into</u> dancing,
O Lord my God, I will <u>thank</u> you for ever.

Fourth Setting

Dom Gregory Murray

I will praise you, Lord, you have res - cued me.

Sing the Psalm tone twice for each verse

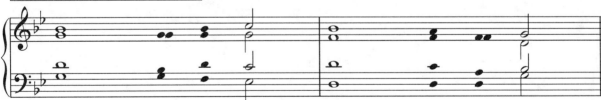

1. I will praise you, Lord, <u>you</u> have rescued me
and have not let my enemies rejoice <u>over</u> me.
O Lord, you have raised my sóul <u>from</u> the dead,
restored me to life from those who sink in<u>to</u> the grave.

2. Sing psalms to the Lord, <u>you</u> who love him,
give thanks to his <u>holy</u> name.
His anger lasts but a moment; his <u>fávour</u> through life.
At night there are tears, but joy <u>comes</u> with dawn.

3. The Lord listened <u>and</u> had pity.
The Lord came <u>to</u> my help.
For me you have changed my mourníng <u>into</u> dancing,
O Lord my God, I will thank <u>you</u> for ever.

The FIFTH READING is taken from Isaiah 55: 1-11

PSALM AFTER THE FIFTH READING
First Setting

Isaiah 12: 2-6

Ian Forrester

1. Truly, God is my salvation,
   I trust, I shall not fear.
   For the Lord is my strength, my song; he became my saviour.
   With joy you will draw water from the wells of salvation.

2. Give thanks to the Lord,
   give praise to his name!
   Make his mighty deeds known to the peoples,
   declare the greatness of his name.

3. Sing a psalm to the Lord for he has done glorious deeds,
   make them known to all the earth!
   People of Zion, sing and shout for joy,
   for great in your midst is the Holy One of Israel.

Second Setting

Dom Gregory Murray

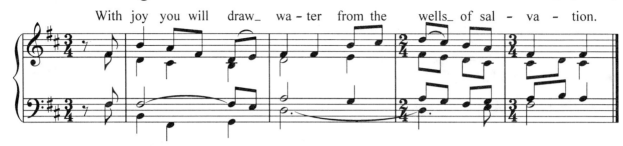

With joy you will draw_ wa-ter from the wells_ of sal - va - tion.

Sing the Psalm tone three times for v 1 and twice for vv 2 & 3

1. Truly God is my salvation,
   I trust, I shall not fear.
   For the Lord is my strength, my song,
   he became my saviour.
   With joy you will draw water
   from the wells of salvation.

2. Give thanks to the Lord,
   give praise to his name!
   Make his mighty deeds known to the peoples,
   declare the greatness of his name.

3. Sing a psalm to the Lord
   for he has done glorious deeds,
   make them known to all the earth!
   People of Zion, sing and shout for joy
   for great in your midst is the Holy One of Israel.

Third Setting

Paschal Jordan

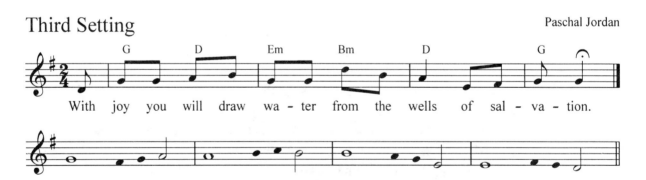

With joy you will draw wa-ter from the wells of sal - va - tion.

1. Truly God is my salvation,
   I trust, I shall not fear.
   For the Lord is my strength, my song,
   he became my saviour.
   With joy you will draw water
   from the wells of salvation.

2. Give thanks to the Lord,
   give praise to his name!
   Make his mighty deeds known to the peoples,
   declare the greatness of his name.

3. Sing a psalm to the Lord
   for he has done glorious deeds,
   make them known to all the earth!
   People of Zion, sing and shout for joy
   for great in your midst is the Holy One of Israel.

For information on copyright, see acknowledgements page

The SIXTH READING is taken from Baruch (3: 9-15, 32 – 4: 4)

PSALM AFTER THE SIXTH READING

Psalm 19 (18): 8-11

First Setting

Paschal Jordan, O.P.

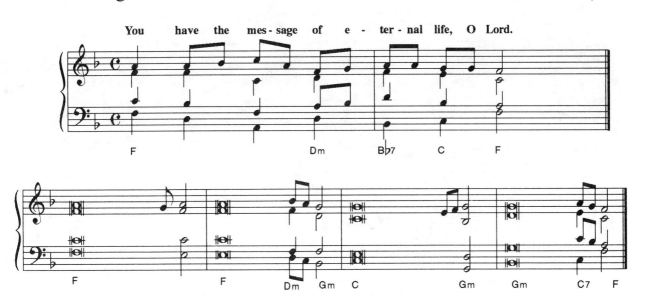

1. The law of the Lord is perfect,
   it revives the soul.
   The rule of the Lord is to be trusted,
   it gives wisdom to the simple.

2. The precepts of the Lord are right
   they gladden the heart.
   The command of the Lord is clear,
   it gives light to the eyes.

3. The fear of the Lord is holy,
   abiding for ever.
   The decrees of the Lord are truth
   and all of them just.

4. They are more to be desired than gold,
   than the purest of gold,
   and sweeter are they than honey,
   than honey from the comb.

Second Setting

Paul Inwood

Third Setting

Orlando Gibbons 1583-1625
arr. Roger Bevan

For information on copyright, see acknowledgements page

Fourth Setting

Paul Davis

1. The law of the Lord is perfect,
   it revives the soul.
   The rule of the Lord is to be trusted,
   it gives wisdom to the simple.

2. The precepts of the Lord are right,
   they gladden the heart.
   The command of the Lord is clear,
   it gives light to the eyes.

3. The fear of the Lord is holy,
   abiding for ever.
   The decrees of the Lord are truth
   and all of them just.

4. They are more to be desired than gold,
   than the purest of gold,
   and sweeter are they than honey,
   than honey from the comb.

Fifth Setting

Dom Gregory Murray

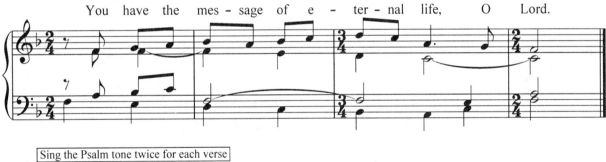

1. The law of the Lord is perfect,
   it revives the soul.
   The rule of the Lord is to be trusted,
   it gives wisdom to the simple.

2. The precepts of the Lord are right,
   they gladden the heart.
   The command of the Lord is clear,
   it gives light to the eyes.

3. The fear of the Lord is holy,
   abiding for ever.
   The decrees of the Lord are truth
   and all of them just.

4. They are more to be desired than gold,
   than the purest of gold,
   and sweeter are they than honey,
   than honey from the comb.

The SEVENTH READING is taken from Ezekiel (36: 16-28)

PSALM AFTER THE SEVENTH READING
First Setting

Psalm 42 (41): 3, 5; 43 (42): 3, 4

Tony Barr

Coda - last time

Fine

God.

Am9   D6   Am7   Em9   F♯7sus4

1. My soul is   thirsting   for God,   the God   of   my   life:
2. These things will   I   re-member   as I   pour   out   my   soul:
3. O send forth your   light and   your truth;   let these   be   my   guide.
4. And I will go to the   altar   of God,   the God   of   my   joy.

Fmaj7   Em7   Cmaj7

1. When can   I   enter and   see   the   face   of God?
2. How I would lead the   re - joi-cing crowd   into   the   house   of God.
3. Let them lead me to   your   ho - ly mountain   to   the   place where   you dwell.
4. My Redeemer, I   will   thank   O   God,   my   God.
      you on the harp,

Am7   Fmaj7   Dm7   Cmaj7   Dm7

Second Setting

A.Gregory Murray, O.S.B.

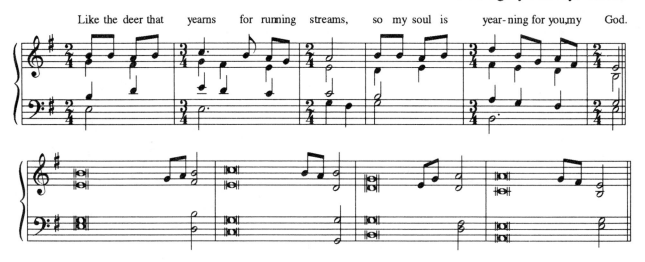

1 My soul is thirsting for God,
   the God of my life;
   when can I enter and see
   the face of God?

2 These things will I remember
   as I pour out my soul:
   how I would lead the rejoicing crowd
   into the house of God,
   amid cries of gladness and thanksgiving,
   the throng wild with joy.

3 O send forth your light and your truth;
   let these be my guide.
   Let them bring me to your holy mountain
   to the place where you dwell.

4 And I will come to the altar of God,
   the God of my joy.
   My redeemer, I will thank you on the harp,
   O God, my God.

Third Setting

Paschal Jordan

Response

Like the deer that yearns for run-ning streams, so my soul is thirs-ting for you my God.

Verses

1 My soul is thirsting for God,
   the God of my life;
   when can I enter and see
   the face of God?

2 These things will I remember
   as I pour out my soul:
   how I would lead the rejoicing crowd
   into the house of God,
   amid cries of gladness and thanksgiving,
   the throng wild with joy.

3 O send forth your light and your truth;
   let these be my guide.
   Let them bring me to your holy mountain
   to the place where you dwell.

4 And I will come to the altar of God,
   the God of my joy.
   My redeemer, I will thank you on the harp,
   O God, my God.

For information on copyright, see acknowledgements page

ALTERNATIVE PSALMS AFTER THE SEVENTH READING

If there are Baptisms, use the Psalm after the Fifth Reading or the Psalm that follows:

First Setting

Psalm 50: 12-15, 18, 19 R v.12

Dom Gregory Murray

Sing the Psalm tone twice for each verse.

1 A pure heart create for <u>me</u>, O God,
   put a steadfast sp<u>irit</u> within me.
   Do not cast me away <u>from</u> your presence,
   nor deprive me of your <u>holy</u> spirit.

2 Give me again the joy <u>of</u> your help;
   with a spirit of fer<u>vour</u> sustain me,
   that I may teach trangre<u>ssors</u> your ways
   and sinners may re<u>turn</u> to you.

3 For in sacrifice you take <u>no</u> delight,
   burnt offering from me you <u>would</u> refuse,
   my sacrifice, a <u>contrite</u> spirit.
   A humbled, contrite heart you <u>will</u> not spurn.

Second Setting

Paschal Jordan

Text of Psalm as for First Setting above.

Third Setting

Ps 51(50):12-15.18.19
Stephen Dean

1. A púre heart creáte for me, O Gód,
   put a stéadfast spírit withín me.
   Do not cást me awáy from your présence,
   nor depríve me of your hóly Spírit.

2. Give me agáin the jóy of your hélp,
   with a spírit of férvour sustáin me,
   that I may téach transgréssors your wáys,
   and sínners may retúrn to yóu.

3. For in sácrifice you táke no delíght
   burnt óffering from mé you would refúse,
   my sácrifice, a cóntrite spírit,
   a húmbled, contrite héart you will not spúrn.

THE MASS OF EASTER NIGHT

After the last reading from the Old Testament with its responsory
and prayer, the altar candles are lighted, and the priest intones the
Gloria, which is taken up by all present. The church bells are rung,
according to local custom.

*(Suggested settings of the Gloria may be found in the Liturgical
Index)*

NEW TESTAMENT READING taken from Romans (6: 3-11)

ALLELUIA

*After the reading from St Paul all rise, and the priest solemnly intones the Alleluia, which is repeated by all
present. The Psalm is then sung. (If necessary the Cantor may intone the Alleluia.) The Responsorial Psalm
follows at once.*

RESPONSORIAL PSALM

An alternative setting of this Psalm can be found on page 171

Ps 118(117):1-2.16-17.22-23
Fintan O'Carroll & Christopher Walker

Al - le - lu - ia, al - le - lu - ia, al - le - lu - ia, al - le - lu - ia.

1. Give thanks to the Lord, he is good.   The love of the Lord knows no
2. The right hand of God raised me up,   the hand of the Lord has
3. The stone which the buil-ders re - jected   be - comes the cor - ner-stone

end-ing.   Sons of Is - ra-el,   say, 'His love has no end'.
tri-umphed.   I shall ne - ver die,   I shall live tell-ing his deeds.
cho-sen.   Praise the work of God   for this marvel in our eyes.

An alternative setting of this Psalm is to be found on p.171

PART THREE: THE LITURGY OF BAPTISM

THE LITANY OF THE SAINTS
First Setting

Dom Gregory Murray

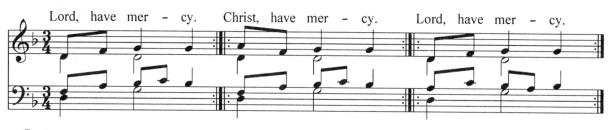

Lord, have mer - cy.   Christ, have mer - cy.   Lord, have mer - cy.

Cantor:
Holy Mary, Mother of   God,   *All:* pray   for   us.

Saint Michael, **pray for us.**	Saint Stephen, **pray for us.**	Saint Martin, **pray for us.**
Holy Angels of God,	Saint Ignatius,	Saint Benedict,
Saint John the Baptist,	Saint Lawrence,	Saint Francis and Saint Dominic,
Saint Joseph,	Saint Perpetua and Saint Felicity,	Saint Francis Xavier
Saint Peter and Saint Paul,	Saint Agnes,	Saint John Vianney,
Saint Andrew,	Saint Gregory,	Saint Catherine,
Saint John,	Saint Augustine,	Saint Theresa,
Saint Mary Magdalen,	Saint Athanasius,	All holy men and women,
	Saint Basil,	

Cantor: Lord, be   merciful. *All:* Lord,   save   your   peo - ple.

From all evil, **Lord, save your people.**   By your coming as man, **Lord, save your people.**
From every sin,   By your death and rising to new life,
From everlasting death   By your gift of the Holy Spirit,

Cantor: Be merciful to us   sinners. *All:* Lord,   hear   our   prayer.

A (Baptisms) *Give new life to these chosen ones by the grace of baptism.* **Lord, hear our prayer.**
B (No Baptisms) *By your grace bless this font where your children will be reborn.* **Lord...**
Jesus, Son of the living God. **Lord...**

Cantor: Christi,___   hear   us.   Lord   Je - sus, *All:* hear   our   prayer.

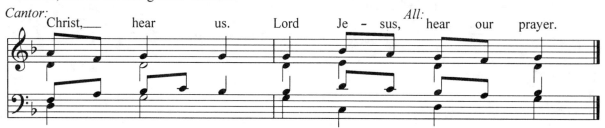

Second Setting

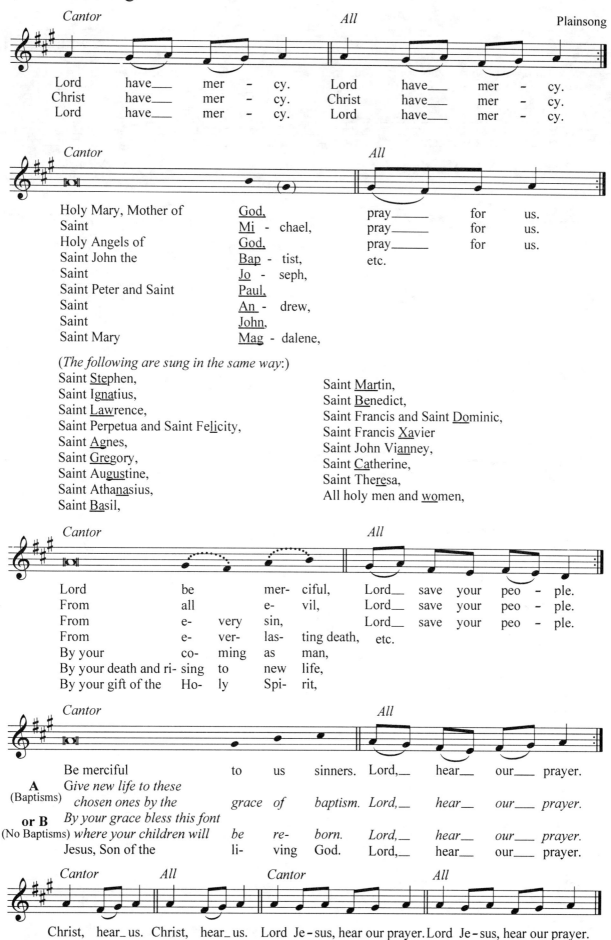

Cantor   *All*   Plainsong

Lord	have__	mer	-	cy.	Lord	have__	mer	-	cy.
Christ	have__	mer	-	cy.	Christ	have__	mer	-	cy.
Lord	have__	mer	-	cy.	Lord	have__	mer	-	cy.

Cantor   *All*

Holy Mary, Mother of	God,	pray_____	for	us.
Saint	Mi - chael,	pray_____	for	us.
Holy Angels of	God,	pray_____	for	us.
Saint John the	Bap - tist,	etc.		
Saint	Jo - seph,			
Saint Peter and Saint	Paul,			
Saint	An - drew,			
Saint	John,			
Saint Mary	Mag - dalene,			

(The following are sung in the same way:)

Saint Stephen,	Saint Martin,
Saint Ignatius,	Saint Benedict,
Saint Lawrence,	Saint Francis and Saint Dominic,
Saint Perpetua and Saint Felicity,	Saint Francis Xavier
Saint Agnes,	Saint John Vianney,
Saint Gregory,	Saint Catherine,
Saint Augustine,	Saint Theresa,
Saint Athanasius,	All holy men and women,
Saint Basil,	

Cantor   *All*

Lord	be	mer-	ciful,	Lord__	save	your	peo	-	ple.
From	all	e-	vil,	Lord__	save	your	peo	-	ple.
From	e-	very	sin,	Lord__	save	your	peo	-	ple.
From	e-	ver-las-	ting death,	etc.					
By your	co-	ming	as	man,					
By your death and ri- sing	to	new	life,						
By your gift of the	Ho-	ly	Spi-	rit,					

Cantor   *All*

	Be merciful	to	us	sinners.	Lord,__	hear__	our__	prayer.
A *Give new life to these*								
(Baptisms) *chosen ones by the*		grace	of	baptism.	Lord,__	hear__	our__	prayer.
or B *By your grace bless this font*								
(No Baptisms) *where your children will*	be	re-	born.	Lord,__	hear__	our__	prayer.	
Jesus, Son of the		li-	ving	God.	Lord,__	hear__	our__	prayer.

Cantor   *All*   *Cantor*   *All*

Christ, hear_us. Christ, hear_us. Lord Je-sus, hear our prayer. Lord Je-sus, hear our prayer.

Third Setting

PART ONE

Paschal Jordan

Cantor: Lord, have mer – cy. Christ, have mer – cy. Lord, have mer – cy.
All: Lord, have mer – cy. Christ, have mer – cy. Lord, have mer – cy.

Cantor: Ho – ly Ma – ry, ho – ly Mo – ther of God; ho – ly Vir – gin of

Vir – gins: pray, pray___ for us. *All:* Pray, pray___ for us. *Cantor:* Saint

Mi – chael and all you An – gels of God:

pray, pray___ for us. *All:* Pray, pray___ for us.

REFRAIN

Cantor: All you Saints of God, by your life and death you pro –

claimed Je – sus Christ as the Light of the World. All you

Saints of God, pray for us. *All:* All you Saints of God, pray for us.

Two Cantors sing alternately
Saint John the Baptist / Saint Joseph
Saint Peter and Saint Paul / Saint Andrew
Saint John / Saint Mary Magdalene

Cantors together
All you Apostles and   Saints,   companions of the   Lord,

pray, pray___ for us. *All:* Pray, pray___ for us.

Sing Refrain

For information on copyright, see acknowledgements page

Two Cantors sing alternately

Saint Stephen / Saint Ignatius
Saint Lawrence / Saint Perpetua and Saint Felicity
Saint Agnes/ (*Holy Martyrs of Uganda*)

Cantors together All you Martyrs and   Saints   witnesses for the   Lord,

pray,   pray___   for   us.   *All:* Pray,   pray___   for   us.
Sing Refrain

Two Cantors sing alternately

Saint Gregory / Saint Augustine
Saint Athanasius / Saint Basil
Saint Martin / Saint Benedict
Saint Bernard / Saint Francis and Saint Dominic
Saint Francis Xavier / Saint John Vianney
Saint Catherine / Saint Theresa

Cantors together All you founders and   Saints,   upbuilding the   Church,

faithful   ser - vants of Christ,   pray,   pray_ for us. *All:* Pray,   pray_ for us.
Sing Refrain

The bracketed section is not part of the official text in the missal and can be omitted.

Two Cantors sing alternately

Saint Vincent de Paul / Saint Martin de Porres
Saint Rose of Lima / Saint Therese of Lisieux

Cantors together
All you men and women   saints,   poor with   Christ,   watch- ing   with Christ,

pray,   pray___   for   us.   *All:* Pray,   pray___   for   us.
Sing Refrain

Two Cantors sing alternately
Saint John Bosco / Saint John Baptist de la Salle
Saint Dominic Savio / Saint Maria Goretti

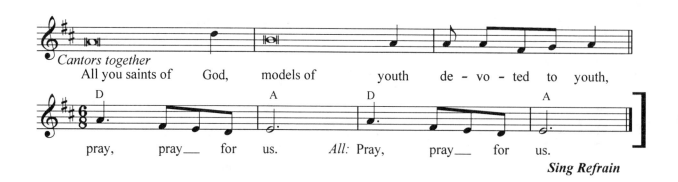

Cantors together
All you saints of God, models of youth de-vo-ted to youth,

pray, pray___ for us. *All:* Pray, pray___ for us.

Sing Refrain

PART TWO

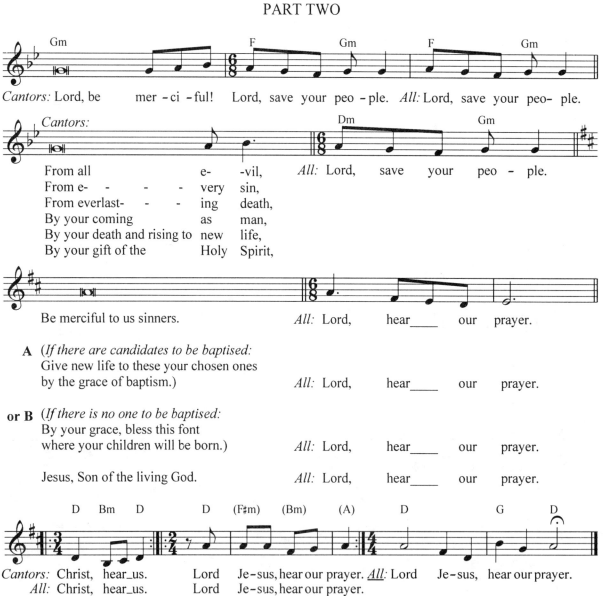

Cantors: Lord, be mer-ci-ful! Lord, save your peo-ple. *All:* Lord, save your peo-ple.

Cantors:

From all e- -vil, *All:* Lord, save your peo-ple.
From e- - - - very sin,
From everlast- - - ing death,
By your coming as man,
By your death and rising to new life,
By your gift of the Holy Spirit,

Be merciful to us sinners. *All:* Lord, hear____ our prayer.

A (*If there are candidates to be baptised:*
Give new life to these your chosen ones
by the grace of baptism.) *All:* Lord, hear____ our prayer.

or B (*If there is no one to be baptised:*
By your grace, bless this font
where your children will be born.) *All:* Lord, hear____ our prayer.

Jesus, Son of the living God. *All:* Lord, hear____ our prayer.

Cantors: Christ, hear_us. Lord Je-sus, hear our prayer. *All:* Lord Je-sus, hear our prayer.
All: Christ, hear_us. Lord Je-sus, hear our prayer.

For information on copyright, see acknowledgements page

Songs and Acclamations for the Rite of Baptism

Grant to us

Lucien Deiss

REFRAIN

Ezekiel 36:26

Grant to us, O Lord, a heart re - newed; re - cre - ate in us your own spi - rit, Lord!

VERSES

Jeremiah 31:34

1. Be - hold, the days are co - ming, says the Lord our God, when I will make a new cov - e - nant with the house of Is - ra - el.

2. Deep wi - thin their be - ing I will im - plant my law; I will write it in their hearts.

3. I will be their God, and they shall be my peo - ple.

4. And for all their faults I will grant for-give-ness; ne-ver more will I re-mem-ber their sins.

G   C   Em   Bm   Em Am   G   C   G

ACCLAMATION AFTER THE BLESSING OF WATER
First Setting

A. Gregory Murray, O.S.B.

Springs of wa-ter, praise the Lord; give him glo-ry and praise for e-ver!

Second Setting

Stephen Dean

This setting may be used in conjunction with the Blessing of Water (no42 in the Missal, RCIA 215). The keyboard or guitar accompaniment is used as a background while the priest proclaims the blessing,, and the sung refrain is inserted at suitable points. After the blessing is finsihed, the refrain may be repeated several times.

Refrain

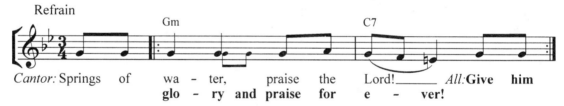

Cantor: Springs of wa-ter, praise the Lord!____ *All:* **Give him glo-ry and praise for e-ver!**

The cantor may add other verses, e.g.:

Seas and rivers, praise the Lord!   Rain and showers ...
Waves and oceans...   Night and darkness..

Keyboard   Choir

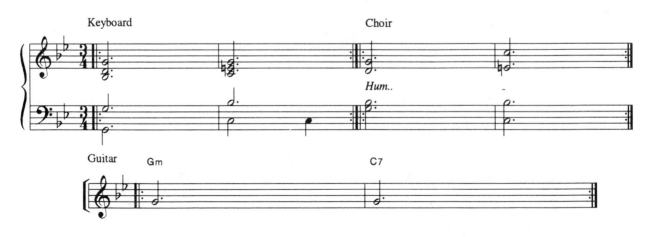

Hum..

Guitar   Gm   C7

Instruments

Third Setting

Lasst uns Erfreuen
(884488 and Alleluias)

Cologne, 1623
arr. Ralph Vaughan Williams (1872-1958)

Unison

Come, flo-wing wa-ter, pure and clear,___ God's Ho-ly Spi-rit bring-ing

Harmony   *Unison*

near,___ Let us praise_ him, al - le - lu - ia! Join___

each to each in peace and love, with life you give us from a-

Harmony

bove.___ O___ praise_ him, O___ praise_ him, al - le -

Unison

lu - ia, al - le - lu - ia,___ al - le - lu - ia.

Words: Author unknown

The Priest sprinkles the people with the blessed water,
while all sing a song which is baptismal in character.

Vidi Aquam
I saw water

Paul Davis

For information on copyright, see acknowledgements page

Optional verse. Psalm (33) 34.9-10.

Taste and see that the Lord is good, they are happy who seek re-fuge in God.

Revere the Lord, you___ saints. They lack no-thing who re-vere the

Lord.

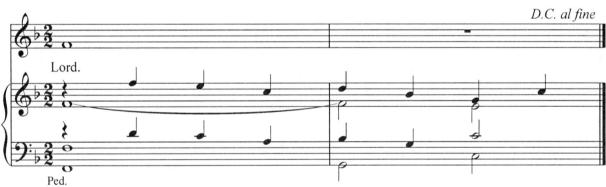

The Dismissal

The Mass is ended, go in peace, al-le-lu - ia, al-le - lu - ia.___
or: Go in the peace of Christ,
or: Go in peace to love and serve the Lord,
or: Ite, Missa est

Thanks be to God,
or: Deo grati- as, al-le-lu - ia, al-le - lu - ia.

Easter Sunday

Processional Song

SALVE FESTA DIES (irregular)

CHORUS

Hail thee, fes-ti-val day! Blest day that art hal-lowed for e - ver;

day where-on Christ a-rose, brea-king the king-dom of death. death. *Fine*

1st time   *To verses*

VERSES *Even and odd-numbered verses are sung alternately after each chorus*

VERSES 2, 4, 6, 8

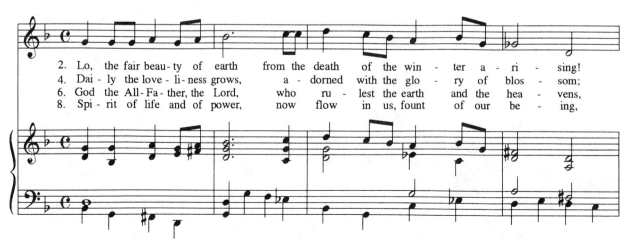

2. Lo, the fair beau-ty of earth from the death of the win - ter a - ri - sing!
4. Dai - ly the love - li - ness grows, a - dorned with the glo - ry of blos - som;
6. God the All-Fa - ther, the Lord, who ru - lest the earth and the hea - vens,
8. Spi - rit of life and of power, now flow in us, fount of our be - ing,

Ev' - ry good gift of the year, now with its Ma-ster re - turns.
hea - ven her gates un - bars, fling - ing her increase of light:
guard us from harm with - out, cleanse us from e - vil with - in:
light that dost ligh - ten all, life that in all dost a - bide:

VERSES 3,5,7,9

3. He who was nailed to the cross is Lord and the ru - ler of all things;
5. Rise from the grave now, O Lord, who art au - thor of life and cre - a - tion.
7. Je - sus the health of the world, en - ligh - ten our minds, thou Re - dee - mer,
9. Praise to the Gi - ver of good! Thou Love who art au - thor of con - cord,

all things cre - a - ted on earth sing to the glo - ry of God:
Trea-ding the path-way of death, life thou be - stow - est on all:
Son of the Fa - ther su - preme, on - ly be - got - ten of God:
pour out thy balm on our souls, or - der our ways in thy peace:

Words: Venantius Fortunatus (530-609)
translated by M.F.Bell
Music:R.Vaughan Williams (1872-1958)

The Lourdes Gloria

Refrain: Jean-Paul Lecot
Verses: Francesca McEvoy
and John Rombaut

Sing refrain after each verse

THE LITURGY OF THE WORD

RESPONSORIAL PSALM

Psalm 117: 1-2, 16-17, 22-23 R v.24 or Alleluia

First Setting

Anthony Milner

RESPONSORIAL PSALM
Second Setting

Stephen Dean

For information on copyright, see acknowledgements page

RESPONSORIAL PSALM
Third Setting

Peter Kielty

RESPONSE

This day was made by the Lord; we re-joice and are glad.

This day was made by the Lord; we re-joice and are

glad!

To verses
After last time, add optional Coda if required

1.Give thanks to the Lord for he is good, for his love has no

end. Let the sons of Is-rael say: 'His love has no end'.

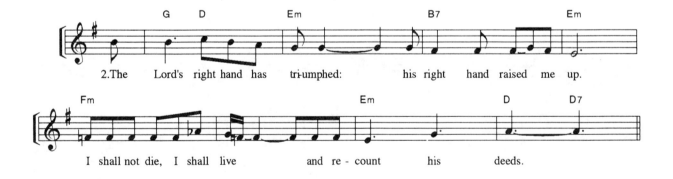

2.The Lord's right hand has tri-umphed: his right hand raised me up.

I shall not die, I shall live and re-count his deeds.

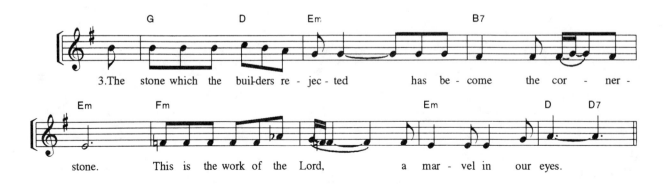

3.The stone which the buil-ders re-jec-ted has be-come the cor-ner-

stone. This is the work of the Lord, a mar-vel in our eyes.

FINAL RESPONSE

This day was made by the Lord,
This day was made by the Lord, we re - joice and are

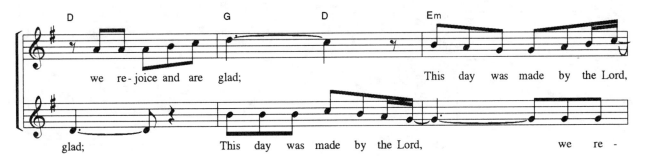

we re - joice and are glad; This day was made by the Lord,
glad; This day was made by the Lord, we re -

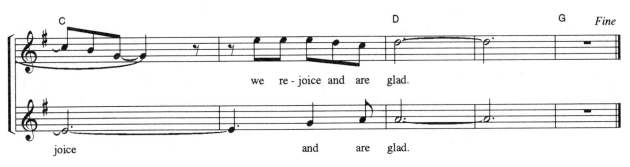

we re - joice and are glad.
joice and are glad.

Fourth Setting

Bernadette Farrell

For information on copyright, see acknowledgements page

SEQUENCE
First Setting

Plainchant

The angels there attesting, shroud with grave clothes resting. Christ my hope has ri - sen:
An - ge - li - cos tes - tes, su - da - ri - um et vestes. Sur - rex - it Chri - stus spes me - a:

he goes be - fore you in - to Ga - li - lee. Tru - ly Christ is raised and li - ving,
prae - ce - det su - os in Ga - li - lae - am. Sci - mus Chri - stum sur - re - xis - se

no death now can touch thim, Vic - to - ri - ous King, thy mer - cy show.
a mor - tu - is ve - re: tu no - bis, vic - tor Rex, mi - se - re - re.

The following ending, though traditional, is not part of the original text and may be omitted:

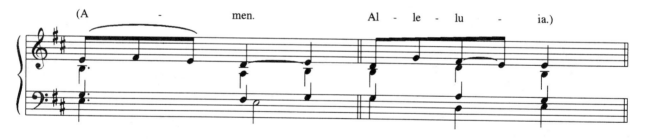

(A - men. Al - le - lu - ia.)

For information on copyright, see acknowledgements page

Second Setting

Vulpius
888 & Alleluias

Melchior Vulpius 1560-1615

1 O Flock of Christ, your ho-mage bring to Christ the Lamb, your glo-rious King! His Eas-ter praise in tri-umph sing! Al-le-lu-ia, al-le-lu-ia, al-le-lu-ia!

2 Peace has come down from God on high!
The King of peace in death did lie!
To save the sheep the Lamb did die!
Alleluia, alleluia, alleluia!

3 Never on earth was stranger sight:
life fought with death in darkest night,
yet lives to reign in endless light!

4 What saw you, Mary, on your way?
'I saw the tomb where Life once lay,
whose glory shone this Easter Day!'

5 'Angels their joyful tidings spread!
Grave-clothes I saw where none lay
    dead,
the cloth that once had veiled his head!'

6 'Christ is my hope, who rose for me!
Soon will you all his glory see!
Christ bids you go to Galilee!'

7 Christ lives again, whose blood was shed,
the Lord of Life, our living Bread,
the Firstborn risen from the dead!

ascribed to Wipo of Burgundy, d. 1048
tr: James Quinn, SJ

Third Setting

Geoffrey Steel

REFRAIN

Verses

1. Chris-tians, to the Pas - chal Vic - tim of-fer sac-ri-fice and praise. The sheep are ran-somed by the Lamb; and Christ, the un-de-filed, hath sinners to his Fa - ther re-con - ciled.

2.Death   with   life   con - ten- ded;   com- bat   strange - ly   en - ded.

Life's   own   cham-pion   slain,   yet   lives   to   reign.

3.Tell   us   Ma - ry: say   what thou didst   see u-pon   the   way.   'The   tomb   the

li - ving did en - close;   I   saw   Christ's   glo-ry as   he   rose;   the   an - gels there at -

tes- ting,   shroud with   grave- clothes   res- ting.   Christ   my   hope   is

ri - sen,   He   goes be-fore you   in - to   Ga-li-lee.

4.   That   Christ   is   ri-sen from   the   dead   we   know: Vic - to -

rious   King,   thy   mer - cy   show,   thy   mer - cy   show.

Refrain - Melody Instrument obbligato

GOSPEL ACCLAMATION

First Setting

Plainsong

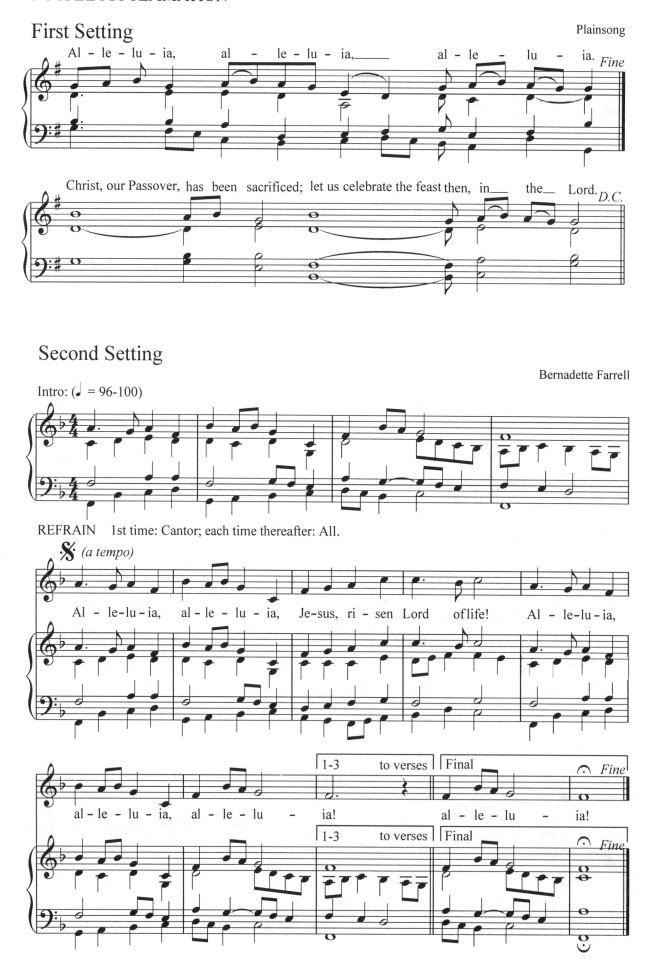

Al - le - lu - ia, al - le - lu - ia,___ al - le - lu - ia. *Fine*

Christ, our Passover, has been sacrificed; let us celebrate the feast then, in___ the_ Lord. *D.C.*

Second Setting

Bernadette Farrell

Intro: (♩ = 96-100)

REFRAIN 1st time: Cantor; each time thereafter: All.

𝄋 (a tempo)

Al - le-lu - ia, al - le-lu - ia, Je-sus, ri - sen Lord of life! Al - le-lu - ia,

1-3 to verses | Final | *Fine*

al - le - lu - ia, al - le - lu - ia! al - le - lu - ia!

For information on copyright, see acknowledgements page

VERSES

Word of the Fa - ther: Je - sus Christ! Hope of the world: Je - sus Christ!

Bro - ken and bu - ried: Je - sus Christ! Ri - sen to life: Je - sus Christ!

2 Light of the nations: **Jesus Christ!**
Way, truth and life: **Jesus Christ!**
Bearing our sorrow: **Jesus Christ!**
With us through time: **Jesus Christ!**

3 Living among us: **Jesus Christ!**
Word in our flesh: **Jesus Christ!**
Servant of others: **Jesus Christ!**
Friend of the poor: **Jesus Christ!**

Third Setting

William Byrd (1542/3-1623) (Ps 55)
arr. Roger Bevan

A SOLO or T.B.   B FULL CHOIR

Al - le - lu - ia.

Al - le - lu - ia. Christ our Passover

Al - le - lu - ia.

Al - le - lu - ia.

has been sac - ri - ficed; let us ce - le - brate the feast then in the Lord.

Repeat Alleluia A, or Alleluia B only.

Fourth Setting

Thomas Tomkins (1573-1656) (Ps 15)
arr. Roger Bevan

Repeat Alleluia A, or Alleluia B only.

Come and praise him

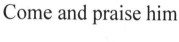

Music: Andy Carter, arr. Andrew Moore
Text: Andy Carter

I saw streams of water flowing

Text and music: Stephen Dean

I saw streams of wa-ter flow - ing from the tem-ple's right side,
hea - ling pow'r and life be - stow - ing from the one who had died: Al - le
lu - ia, al - le - lu - ia, from our Sa - viour glo - ri - fied.

1st time only | To verses | Last time
Fine

1. In - to day from dee - pest night, out of dark - ness in - to light, Christ our
Sa - viour comes once more, o - pens up sal - va - tion's door!

D.C.

2 He has healed us with his blood,
led us safe through Jordan's flood,
on the further bank we stand,
gazing on the promised land!

3 He has raised us from the grave,
from the Red Sea's mighty wave;
dead to sin we rise with Christ,
Paschal Lamb now sacrificed.

Surrexit Christus

Jacques Berthier

MIXED VOICES

(hum)

Sur - re - xit Chris - tus, al - le - lu - ia!

(hum)

Can - ta - te Do - mi - no, al - le - lu - ia!

Choir Variation for B & C

Sur - re - xit Chris - tus, al - le - lu - ia!

Can - ta - te Do - mi - no, al - le - lu - ia!

Keyboard/Guitar

VERSES (Cantor)

From Daniel 3 (The praises of creation)

1.All you hea - vens, bless the Lord.   Stars of the hea - vens,

For information on copyright, see acknowledgements page

bless the Lord.   2.Sun and moon, bless the Lord,

And you, night and day, bless the Lord.

3.Frost and cold, bless the Lord.   Ice and snow, bless the Lord.

4.Fire and heat, bless the Lord.   And

you, light and dark-ness, bless the Lord.   5.Spi-rits and souls of the

just, bless the Lord.   Saints and the hum-ble hear-ted, bless the Lord.

From Ps 118 (117)

1.Give thanks to the Lord, for he is good,   for his love

has no end.   2.The Lord is my strength, the Lord is my song,

he has been my Sa - viour.

3.I shall not die,   I shall live,

I shall live and re - count his deeds.

Copyright Acknowledgements

Details of copyright holders

Psalm texts from the Roman Missal are © The Grail (see below)
Other excerpts from the Missal are © ICEL (see below)

AINSLIE, John, 76 Great Bushey Drive, Totteridge, London, N20 8QL, for *The Glory of the Cross* p21.

ATELIERS et Presses de TAIZÉ, F-71250 Taizé-Communauté, France, for *Hosanna* p8, *Ubi Caritas* p38, *Eat this Bread* p43, *Bleibet Hier (Stay with me)* p52, *Stay here and keep watch* p53, *Jesus Remember me* p107, *Crucem Tuam* p108, *Surrexit Christus* p190.

AMPLEFORTH ABBEY TRUST, The Procurator's Office, Ampleforth College, York YO62 4EY, for *I will praise you Lord* p145.

BEVAN, Roger, c/o Continuum International Publishing Group Ltd., The Tower Building, 11 York Road, London SE1 7NX, for the arrangements of: GIBBONS: *Lord you have the message* p150, BYRD: *Alleluia* p187, TOMKINS: *Alleluia* p188.

CJM MUSIC, St Mary's House, Coventry Road, Coleshill, West Midlands B46 3ED, for *Veronica's Litany* p110.

CHRISTIAN MUSIC MINISTRIES, 325 Bromford Road, Hodge Hill, Birmingham B36 8ET, for *When I survey* (music) p112.

COLEMAN, Ian, 29 Churston Gardens, London N11 2NJ, for *Praise to you* p20, *Father into your hands* p56.

DAVIS, Paul, 125 Hillcrest Road, Orpington, Kent BR6 9AG, for *Pueri Hebraeorum* (accompaniment) p13, *My God* (music of response & verse) p16, *The blessing cup* p25, *Ubi caritas* (accompaniment) p41, *Je suis le maitre* (arrangement) p47, hymn tunes *Leinthall Starkes* p87 and *Santeuil* p101, *The Lord fills the earth* and psalm verse (music) p135, *You have the message* p151, *Vidi Aquam* and psalm verse (music) p166. Copyrights administered by McCrimmon Publishing Co. Ltd.

DARTON, LONGMAN & TODD, 89 Lillie Road, London SW6 1UD, for biblical texts taken from the *Jerusalem Bible*, published and copyright 1966, 1967 and 1968 by Darton, Longman and Todd Ltd and Doubleday & Co. Inc and used by the permission of the publishers.

DEAN, Stephen, Decani Music, 30 North Terrace, Mildenhall, Suffolk IP28 7AB, for *Hosanna* p3, *Come to Jerusalem* (adaptation of words) p11, *Glory and praise* p19, *Our blessing cup* p22, *Praise and honour* p27, *Father into your hands* p54, *Rejoice to greet* p126, *Evening came* p130, *Send forth* p132, *I will sing* p142, *I will praise you* p145, *Springs of water* p164, *This day* p172.

FORRESTER, Ian, The Priory Vicarage, Church Lane, Boxgrove, Chichester, West Sussex, PO18 0ED, for *With joy you will draw water* p147.

GIA PUBLICATIONS Inc. 7404 S. Mason Ave., Chicago, Illinois 60638, for *There is no greater Love* p34.

GLYNN, John, Abbotswick, Navestock Side, Brentwood, Essex, CM14 5SH, for *Preserve me, God* p136.

THE GRAIL, c/o Lesley Toll, 23 Castle Road, London NW6 6TL, for the texts of the Psalms.

INTERNATIONAL COMMITTEE ON ENGLISH IN THE LITURGY Inc., 1275 K Street NW, Suite 1022, Washington D.C., 2005-4097, for the text of *Hosanna to the Son of David*, *Where is Love and Loving Kindness*, *This is the wood of the cross*, *The Reproaches*, *Exsultet*, excerpts from the Roman Missal c 1973. All rights reserved.

INWOOD, Paul, Park Place Pastoral Centre, Winchester Road, Wickham, Hants, PO17, for *Lord in your mercy* p59

IONA COMMUNITY WGRG, Iona Community, 840 Govan Road, Glasgow, G51 3UU, for *Though one with God* (words) p20.

JABULANI MUSIC/TONY BARR, 4784 Riverwood Drive N, Keizer OR 97303, USA, for *Praise to you* p58.

KIELTY, Peter, for *This day was made by the Lord* p174.

KINGSLEY, David c/o Paul Inwood, for *The Reproaches* p64.

KINGSWAY THANKYOU, Loftbridge Drive, Eastbourne, East Sussex, BN23 6NT, for *Draw me close* p84, *Come and praise* p188.

LILLIS, John, Cartref, Kingfield Road, Woking, Surrey, GU22 9EQ, for *Christ was humbler yet* p19.

MACARDLE, Fiona, 9 Springfield Road, Durham, DH1 4LS, for *Into your hands* p55.

KEVIN MAYHEW LTD, Buxhall, Stowmarket, Suffolk IP14 3DJ, for *Lauda Jerusalem* p14, Rees: *Where is Love* (music) p40, *My soul is sad* p53, *My people* p66, *O my people* p78, *I give you love* p80, *My people* p81, *Rejoice all heavenly powers* (words) p127. *Lourdes Gloria*, refrain only p170.

McEVOY, Fran, 25 Fairmead Avenue, Westcliff-on-Sea, Essex, for *Lourdes Gloria* music for verses (with John Rombaut) p170

MUSTARD SEED MUSIC, P.O. Box 356, Leighton Buzzard, LU7 8WP, for *Broken for me* p42.

NOVELLO & CO., 8-9 Frith Street, London W1V 5TZ, for Stainer: *God so loved the world* p102

O'HARA, Chris, 53 Pikes Lane, Glossop, Yorks, SK13 8ED, for *Glory & praise to you* p28, *My people* p74.

OREGON CATHOLIC PRESS, 5536 N.E. Hassalo, Portland, Oregon, 97213-3638 for
(1) BARR, Tony, *Hosanna* p3, *Like the deer* p152;
(2) DEAN, Stephen, *Father if this cup* p44, *The bread that we break* p46, and *I saw streams of*

water flowing p189; (3) FARRELL, Bernadette, *The Stone which the builders rejected* p176, *Alleluia Jesus Risen Lord* p186; (4) INWOOD, Paul, *Lord in your mercy* p59, *This is the wood* p62, *Keep me safe* p137, *You Lord have the message* p149; (5) JONES, Peter, *O my people* p68; (6) WALKER, Christopher, *The blessing cup* p26, *Evening came* p130, *Preserve me God* p138, *Celtic Alleluia* p157, *Like the Deer* p152.

QUINN, Fr James, S.J., c/o Continuum International Publishing Group Ltd., The Tower Building, 11 York Road, London, SE1 7NX, for *O Flock of Christ* (words) p183.

ROMBAUT, John, 65 Olivia Drive, Leigh-on-Sea, Essex, SS9 3EF, for *Hosanna* p7, *The Reproaches* p82, *Pie Jesu* p100, *The Lourdes Gloria* music for verses p170 (with Francesca McEvoy).
* Administered by McCrimmon Publishing Co. Ltd.

OXFORD UNIVERSITY PRESS, Ely House, 37 Dover Street, London, W1X 4AH, for the tunes *Gonfalon Royal* p88, and *Lasst uns erfreunen* p165, *Hail thee Festival Day* (words) p168, and the tune *Salve Festa Dies* p168.

ROYAL SCHOOL OF CHURCH MUSIC, Cleveland Lodge, Westhumble Street, Westhumble, Dorking, Surrey, RH15 6BW, for *Come, Christ's Beloved* (words and arrangement) p48, (melody © James Walsh, see below.)

ST. BENEDICT'S FARM, P.O. Box 366, Waelder, Texas, 78959, for *Chosen people of the Lord* p12.

STEEL, Geoffrey, St Augustine of Canterbury, St Austin's Place, Preston, PR1 3YJ, for *Victimae Pashcale Laudes* p184.

WALSH, James, 468 Norwich Road, Ipswich, Suffolk IP1 6JS, for *Come Christ's Beloved* (melody) p48, & see RSCM above, *Glory and praise* to you p57.

WARD, Anne, 2 Goodacres, Arundel Road, Fontwell, West Sussex, BN18 0SF, for *My God* p18, *The Lord fills the earth* p134.

WESTON PRIORY PRODUCTIONS, Weston, Vermont 05161, for Gregory Norbet: *The Lord Jesus* p30.

WORLD LIBRARY PUBLICATIONS, 3815 North Willow Road, Schiller Park, Illinois, 60176, for Lucien Diess: *Grant to us* p163.

McCRIMMON PUBLISHING COMPANY LTD., *Hosanna* (2 settings) p6, *The Children of Jerusalem* p10, *When the people heard* p11, *My God* p15, *My God* p16, *The blessing cup* p24, *The blessing cup* p25, *O Jesus you are the word of God* p28, *The Lord Jesus* p29, *I give you* p29, *A new commandment* (arrangement) p32, *Lord do you wash my feet?* p33, *Pange Lingua* (arrangement) p51, *My soul is sad* (arrangement) p53, *Father into your hands* p54 & p56, *Christ was humbler yet* p59, *This is the wood* p60 & p61, *The Reproaches* p70, *The Reproaches* p73, *O my people* (arrangement) p78, *Ecrit au bas D'un Crucifix* p86, *Palestrina: Adoramus te* (edition) p90, *Croce: O vos omnes* (edition) p92, MOZART: *Ave verum* (edition)

p94, FAURE: *Pie Jesu* (edition) p97, *Christ our Light* (settings 2 3 & 4) p118, *Exsultet* p122 & p128, *Send forth* (2 settings) p131, *Preserve me* (2 settings) p140, *I will sing* p141, *I will sing* (2 settings) p144, *I will praise you* (2 settings) p146, *With joy* (2 settings) p148, *You have the message* p149 (Jordan) & p151 (Murray), *A pure heart* p155, *Create for me* p155, *Litany* p158 & p160, *Springs of water* (Murray) p164, MILNER: *Alleluia* p171.

A note on copyright

Index of first lines and copyright holders

Psalm texts from the Roman Missal are
© The Grail (see below)
Other excerpts from the Missal are
© ICEL (see below)

Titles in italics
Arr. = Arrangement

First line	Copyright holder	Page no.
A new commandment	McC	p32
A pure heart create for me (Dean)	❖	156
A pure heart create for me (Murray)	McC	155
Adoramus te, Christe (Palestrina)	McC	90
Agios, O Theos (Trisagion)		79
All glory, laud and honour		9
Alleluia (O'Carroll/Walker)	❖/OCP	157
Alleluia (Plainchant) *1st Alleluia of Easter*	Arr: McC	156
Alleluia (Plainsong/Milner)	Arr: McC	171
Alleluia, alleluia, Jesus, risen Lord	❖/OCP	186
Alleluia. Christ our Passover (Byrd)	BV	187
Alleluia. Christ our Passover (Plainsong)	Arr: McC	186
Alleluia. Christ our Passover (Tomkins)	BV	188
Ave verum (Mozart)	Edition: McC	94
Behold, behold	*Not traced*	61
Bread of the world	Arr: P. Davis	47
Broken for me	MS	42
Celtic Alleluia	❖/OCP	157
Chosen people of the Lord	St BF	12
Christ our light Settings 2 3 & 4	McC	118
Christ was humbler yet (Milner)	McC	59
Christ was humbler yet (Lillis)	❖	19
Christians to the Paschal victim	Arr: McC	181
Come and praise him	KT	188
Come to Jerusalem	Text: SD	11
Come, Christ's beloved		
Words & arr: RSCM. Melody: WH		48
Come, flowing water	Music: OUP	165
Create for me a humble heart	McC	155
Crucem tua	TZ	108
Draw me close to the Cross	KT	84
Drop, drop slow tears (Gibbons)		99
Eat this bread	TZ	43
Ecrit au bas d'un Crucifix	McC	86
Evening came (Dean)	❖	130
Evening came (Walker)	❖/OCP	130
Exsultet (Murray)	Music: McC. Text: ICEL	122
Exsultet (Plainsong)	ICEL	119
Exsultet (Rochard)	McC	128
Father, if this cup (Dean)	❖/OCP	44

First line	Copyright holder	Page no.
Father, into your hands (Coleman)	❖	56
Father, into your hands (Dean)	❖	54
Father, into your hands (Jordan)	McC	56
Father, into your hands (Murray)	McC	54
Gloria (Lourdes)	Refrain: KM. Verses: McE&R	170
Glory and praise to you (Dean)	❖	19
Glory and praise to you (O'Hara)	❖	28
Glory and praise to you (Walsh)	❖	57
God so loved the world (Stainer)	NV	102
Grant to us, O Lord	WLP	163
Hail thee, festival day	OUP	168
Hosanna	TZ	8
Hosanna filio David (Terry)		4
Hosanna to the Son of David (Barr)	❖/OCP	3
Hosanna to the Son of David (Dean)	❖	3
Hosanna to the Son of David (Mayhew Bb)	McC	6
Hosanna to the Son of David (Mayhew G)	McC	6
Hosanna to the Son of David (Rombaut)	❖/McC	7
I give you a new commandment	McC	29
I give you love (Forster)	Text: KM. Music: BH	80
I saw streams (Dean)	❖/OCP	189
I saw water (Davis)	Music: ❖	166
I will praise you, Lord (Benevot)	❖ Exec.	145
I will praise you, Lord (Jordan)	McC	146
I will praise you, Lord (Murray)	McC	146
I will praise you, Lord (O'Carroll/Dean)	SD	145
I will sing to the Lord (Abraham)	McC	141
I will sing to the Lord (Dean)	❖	142
I will sing to the Lord (Milner)	McC	144
I will sing to the Lord (Murray)	McC	144
Into your hands, O Lord (Macardle)	❖	55
Ite, Missa est (Easter Alleluia)	Arr: McC	162
Jesus, remember me	TZ	107
Jesus, you are the word of God	McC	28
Keep me safe, O God	❖/OCP	137
Lauda Jerusalem	KM	14
Like the deer that yearns (Barr)	❖/OCP	152
Like the deer that yearns (Jordan)	McC	154
Like the deer that yearns (Murray)	McC	154
Litany (Jordan)	McC	160
Litany (Murray)	McC	158
Litany (Plainsong)	ICEL	159
Lord, do you wash my feet?	McC	33
Lord, in your mercy	❖/OCP	59
Lord, you have the message (Gibbons)	BV	150
Lourdes Gloria	Refrain: KM. Verses: McE&R	170
My God, my God (Davis)	❖	16
My God, my God (Laugier)	McC	16
My God, my God (Milner)	McC	15
My God, my God (Ward)	❖	18
My Lord, my master	❖	87
My people - *The Reproaches* (Jones)	❖/OCP	68

First line	Copyright holder	Page no.
My people - *The Reproaches* (Jordan)	McC	73
My people - *The Reproaches* (Kingsley)	❖	64
My people - *The Reproaches* (Mayhew)	KM	66
My people - *The Reproaches* (Milner)	McC	70
My people - *The Reproaches* (O'Hara)	❖	74
My people - *The Reproaches* (Rombaut)	❖/McC	82
My people - *The Reproaches* (Leftly)	KM	81
My soul is sad	Tune & text: KM	53
No greater love	GIA	34
Now my soul	Music: P.Davis	101
O flock of Christ	Text: Quinn	183
O my people - *The Reproaches* (Lundy)	KM	78
O vos omnes (Croce)	Edition: McC	92
Of the glorious body telling (Picardy)		50
Of the glorious body telling (St Thomas)		49
Our blessing cup	SD	22
Pange lingua	Accomp: McC	51
Pie Jesu (Faure)	Edition: McC	97
Pie Jesu (Rombaut)	❖/McC	100
Praise and honour to you	SD	27
Praise to you, Lord Jesus (Barr)	JM	58
Praise to you, O Christ	IC	20
Preserve me, God (Glynn)	❖	136
Preserve me, God (Jordan)	McC	140
Preserve me, God (Murray)	McC	140
Preserve me, God (Walker)	❖/OCP	138
Pueri Hebraeorum	Accomp: P. Davis	13
Rejoice, all heavenly powers	Text: KM	127
Rejoice, heavenly powers – *see Exsultet*		
Reproaches – see 'My people'		
Send forth your Spirit, O Lord (Dean)	❖	132
Send forth your Spirit, O Lord (Jordan)	McC	131
Send forth your Spirit, O Lord (Murray)	McC	131
Springs of water (Dean)	❖	164
Springs of water (Murray)	McC	164
Stay here and keep watch	TZ	53
Stay with me	TZ	52
Surrexit Christus	TZ	190
The blessing-cup (Davis)	❖	25
The blessing-cup (Murray)	McC	24
The blessing-cup (Rochard)	McC	25
The blessing-cup (Walker)	❖/OCP	26
The bread that we break	❖/OCP	46
The Children of Jerusalem	McC	10
The Dismissal (Easter Alleluia)		162
The glory of the Cross	JA	21
The Lord fills the earth (Davis)	❖	135
The Lord fills the earth (Ward)	❖	134
The Lord Jesus (Murray)	McC	29
The Lord Jesus (Norbert)	WP	30
The Mass is ended (Easter Alleluia)	Arr: McC	162
The royal banners forward go	Music: OUP	88

First line	Copyright holder	Page no.
The stone which the builders rejected	❖/OCP	176
There is no greater love	GIA	34
This day was made by the Lord (Dean)	❖	172
This day was made by the Lord (Kielty)	❖	174
This is wood of the Cross (Inwood)	❖/OCP	62
This is wood of the Cross (Jordan)	McC	60
This is wood of the Cross (Murray)	McC	60
Though one with God	Words: Iona	20
Trisagion		79
Ubi caritas (Plainsong)	Accomp: P.Davis	41
Ubi caritas	TZ	38
Veronica's Litany	CJM	110
Vexilla regis		89
Victimae paschali laudes (Plainsong)	Accomp: McC	181
Victimae paschali laudes (Steel)	❖	184
Vidi aquam	Music: PD	166
Vous qui pleurez	McC	86
What have they done to you, Lord?	CJM	110
What wondrous love	Text: ICEL, Arr. SD	109
When I survey	Music: CMM	112
When the people heard	McC	11
Where is love	Music: KM	40
With joy you will draw water (Forrester)	❖	147
With joy you will draw water (Jordan)	McC	148
With joy you will draw water (Murray)	McC	148
You have the message (Davis)	❖	151
You have the message (Jordan)	McC	149
You have the message (Murray)	McC	151
You, Lord, have the message (Inwood)	❖/OCP	149
You who mourn	McC	86

Liturgical Index

Indicating suitable hymns from
CELEBRATION HYMNAL
FOR EVERYONE

Palm Sunday
PROCESSION OF PALMS
You are the King of Glory 822

Processional and Hosannas
Hosanna, blessed is he 264
Hosanna, loud hosanna 265
Ride on, ride on in majesty 623
We cry hosanna, Lord 775
Jesus, the holy Lamb of God . . . 330
or other suitable hymn to Christ the King

PREPARATION OF THE GIFTS AND COMMUNION SONGS
Ah, holy Jesus 13
I met you at the cross 279
Feed my lambs 170
From the depths 188
My Lord what love is this 500
My song is love unknown 503
O sacred head (Bach) 552
Ours were the sins 589
Ours were the sufferings 590

RECESSIONAL
Crown him with many crowns . . 139
From heaven you came 187
Hail redeemer, King divine 239

Maundy Thursday
PROCESSIONAL
Love is his word 399
Meekness and majesty 487
O thou who at thy Eucharist 556

GLORIA
Mass of Peace 405
Gloria (Salazar) 406
Coventry Gloria 407
Gloria (Philip Duffy) 409
Missa de Angelis 467

GOSPEL ACCLAMATION
A new commandment 4

WASHING OF THE FEET
An upper room 42
God is love (Ubi Caritas) 214
Into one we all are gathered 312
  (Ubi Caritas)
I have loved you 276
Into one we all are gathered 312
Jesu, Jesu 318
This is my will 732
Where is love 809

PREPARATION OF THE GIFTS AND COMMUNION SONGS
Jesus my Lord, my God 329
Bread, blessed and broken 334
O bread of heaven 517
O Father, take in sign of love . . . 524
O King of might and splendour . 537
One bread, one body 578
Sweet Sacrament divine 674
Taste and see 682
The heavenly word 697
The green life rises 695
This is what Yahweh asks 734
When the time came 807
The Servant song 813

ADORATION
O come and mourn with me
  awhile 521

Good Friday
Ah holy Jesus, how hast thou
  offended 13
Dear love of my heart 144
Feed my lambs 170
From the depths of sin 188
Glory be to Jesus 197
I met you at the cross 279
Jesus the holy Lamb of God 330
Lift high the Cross 363
My Lord, what love is this? 500
My song is love unknown 503
O come and mourn with me
  awhile 521
O sacred head 552
The old rugged Cross 573

Ours were the sins 589
Ours were the sufferings 590
Sing my tongue 650
There is a green hill 721
They hung him on a cross 727
Were you there? 791
When I survey the wondrous
  cross 801

The Easter Vigil
THE SERVICE OF LIGHT
The light of Christ (refrain only) . . 703

LITURGY OF THE WORD
2nd Reading
Centre of my life 543

5th Reading
We shall draw water joyfully . . . 787

6th Reading
The Word of God 720

7th Reading
As the deer longs 53
As the deer pants 54
Like as the deer yearns 370

Gloria
  (See Maundy Thursday)

Responsorial Psalm
after the Epistle
Alleluia! This is the day 38

LITURGY OF BAPTISM
God at creation's dawn 204
God, our fountain of salvation . . 221

Acclamation after the blessing
of the water
Water of life (chorus only) 401

Blessing of the congregation
with Holy Water
Called to be servants 104
Flow river flow 155
God at creation's dawn 204
Water of life 401
O praise ye the Lord 547
O wash me 558
O healing river 565
Out of deep unordered water . . . 592
You have put on Christ 825

CONFIRMATION

Officially there is no place in the rite for a Confirmation song, only for one of a 'baptismal nature' to be sung when the people are sprinkled with Holy Water.

All hail the Lamb 18

All heaven declares. 20

Alleluia, Alleluia, give thanks. . . . 32

At the Lamb's high feast. 58

Breathe on me, breath of God. . . . 98

Come Holy Ghost. 126

Holy Spirit of fire 262

Jesus is Lord. 326

Join in the dance 333

Lamb of God 345

Laudate Dominum 346

Now the green blade rises. 513

O Jesus, I have promised 536

O living water. 566

Sing of the Lord's goodness 654

Spirit of the living God. 666

Surrexit Christus. 672

The gift of the Holy Spirit 693

This joyful Eastertide 735

Behold the Lamb of God 737

Veni Sancte Spiritus *(chorus only)* 759

We have a Gospel to proclaim . . 778

Servant song 795

Holy Spirit, we welcome you S6

RECESSIONAL

Christ the Lord is risen today . . . 112

Jesus Christ is risen today. 322

The day of Resurrection 690

Thine be the glory. 728

Easter Sunday

PROCESSIONAL

Battle is o'er 68

Bring, all ye dear-bought nations 100

Christ the Lord is risen today . . . 112

Good Christians all 230

Jesus Christ is risen. 322

The day of Resurrection 690

Ye sons and daughters of
the Lord. 820

GLORIA

As for Maundy Thursday, also:
Gloria (Anderson). 408

RESPONSORIAL PSALM

Alleluia! This is the day 38

Celtic Alleluia. 410

SEQUENCE

Bring, all ye dear-bought nations 100

Christ the Lord is risen today . . . 112

Jesus Christ is risen today. 322

GOSPEL ACCLAMATION

Celtic Alleluia. 410
(with Easter verse)

RENEWAL OF BAPTISMAL PROMISES

Firmly I believe and truly 173
If the Creed is to be sung, Easter is an ideal time to use Credo III.
Credo III 469

PREPARATION OF GIFTS AND COMMUNION SONGS

Songs as listed for the EASTER VIGIL and the following:

He is Lord. 246

He is risen. 247

Keep in mind 340

Sing a new song unto the Lord . . 644

Sing a new song to the Lord 645

Sing to the mountains 657

The day of Resurrection 690

The King of glory 698

This is the day. 731

Ye choirs of new Jerusalem 818

Ye sons and daughters of
the Lord 820

Index of first lines

Titles in italics

A new commandment 32

A pure heart create for me (Dean) 156

A pure heart create for me (Murray)..................155

Adoramus te, Christe (Palestrina) 90

Agios, O Theos (Trisagion)...........................79

All glory, laud and honour 9

Alleluia (O'Carroll/Walker) 157

Alleluia (Plainsong) 1st Alleluia of Easter 156

Alleluia (Plainsong/Milner)............................171

Alleluia, alleluia, Jesus, risen Lord..................186

Alleluia. Christ our Passover (Byrd).................187

Alleluia. Christ our Passover (Plainsong)..........186

Alleluia. Christ our Passover (Tomkins)............188

Ave verum (Mozart)....................................94

Behold, behold the wood of the Cross.................61

Bread of the world.......................................47

Broken for me 42

Celtic Alleluia.. 157

Chosen people of the Lord................................12

Christ our light 118

Christ was humbler yet (Milner).......................59

Christ was humbler yet (Lillis) 19

Christians to the Paschal victim (Sequence)......181

Come and praise him....................................188

Come to Jerusalem 11

Come, Christ's beloved 48

Come, flowing water.....................................165

Create for me a humble heart.........................155

Crucem tuam (Taizé).....................................108

Draw me close to the Cross 84

Drop, drop slow tears (Gibbons)........................99

Eat this bread...43

Ecrit au bas d'un Crucifix...............................86

Evening came (Dean)....................................130

Evening came (Walker)..................................130

Exsultet (Murray) 122

Exsultet (Plainsong)....................................119

Exsultet (Rochard)......................................128

Father, if this cup...44

Father, into your hands (Coleman)....................56

Father, into your hands (Dean)........................54

Father, into your hands (Jordan) 56

Father, into your hands (Murray)......................54

Gloria (Lourdes)..170

Glory and praise to you (Dean)........................19

Glory and praise to you (O'Hara)......................28

Glory and praise to you (Walsh) 57

God so loved the world (Stainer)......................102

Grant to us, O Lord.......................................163

Hail thee, festival day....................................168

Hosanna (Taizé)..8

Hosanna filio David (Terry)..............................4

Hosanna to the Son of David (Barr) 3

Hosanna to the Son of David (Dean)...................3

Hosanna to the Son of David (Mayhew Bb)..........6

Hosanna to the Son of David (Mayhew G) 6

Hosanna to the Son of David (Rombaut)..............7

I give you a new commandment.........................29

I give you love *The Reproaches* (Forster)...........80

I saw streams of water flowing (Dean).............189

I saw water (*Vidi aquam*) 166

I will praise you, Lord (Benevot).....................145

I will praise you, Lord (Jordan) 146

I will praise you, Lord (Murray)......................146

I will praise you, Lord (O'Carroll/Dean)...........145

I will sing to the Lord (Abraham)....................141

I will sing to the Lord (Dean) 142

I will sing to the Lord (Milner)........................144

I will sing to the Lord (Murray).......................144

Into your hands, O Lord (Macardle).................55

Ite, Missa est (Easter Alleluia) 162

Jesus, remember me (Taizé)............................107

Jesus, you are the word of God........................28

Keep me safe, O God....................................137

Lauda Jerusalem...14

Let us go forth..9

Like the deer that yearns (Barr).......................152

Like the deer that yearns (Jordan)....................154

Like the deer that yearns (Murray) 154

Litany (Jordan)..160

Litany (Murray)...158

Litany (Plainsong) 159

Lord, do you wash my feet?............................33

Lord, in your mercy 59

Lord, you have the message (Gibbons) 150

Lourdes Gloria 170

My God, my God (Davis) 16

My God, my God (Laugier) 16

My God, my God (Milner) 15

My God, my God (Ward) 18

My Lord, my master 87

My people – *The Reproaches* (Jones) 68

My people – *The Reproaches* (Jordan) 73

My people – *The Reproaches* (Kingsley) 64

My people – *The Reproaches* (Mayhew)............66

My people – *The Reproaches* (Milner) 70

My people – *The Reproaches* (O'Hara).............74

My people – *The Reproaches* (Rombaut) 82

My people – *The Reproaches* (Leftly) 81

My soul is sad 53

No greater love 34

Now my soul, thy voice upraising 101

O flock of Christ 183

O my people – *The Reproaches* (Lundy)............78

O vos omnes (Croce)..92

Of the glorious body telling (Picardy) 50

Of the glorious body telling (St Thomas) 49

Our blessing cup..22

Pange lingua 51

Pie Jesu (Faure) 97

Pie Jesu (Rombaut) 100

Praise and honour to you..................................27

Praise to you, Lord Jesus 58

Praise to you, O Christ 20

Preserve me, God (Glynn) 136

Preserve me, God (Jordan)................................140

Preserve me, God (Murray) 140

Preserve me, God (Walker) 138

Pueri Hebraeorum 13

Rejoice, all heavenly powers 127

Rejoice, heavenly powers. See: 'Exsultet'

Reproaches – See: 'My people'

Send forth your Spirit, O Lord (Dean)................132

Send forth your Spirit, O Lord (Jordan) 131

Send forth your Spirit, O Lord (Murray)...........131

Springs of water (Dean) 164

Springs of water (Murray).................................164

Stay here and keep watch (Taizé) 53

Stay with me (Taizé) 52

Surrexit Christus (Taizé) 190

The blessing-cup (Davis) 25

The blessing-cup (Murray)................................24

The blessing-cup (Rochard) 25

The blessing-cup (Walker) 26

The bread that we break....................................46

The Children of Jerusalem 10

The Dismissal (Easter Alleluia).........................162

The glory of the Cross......................................21

The Lord fills the earth (Davis) 135

The Lord fills the earth (Ward) 134

The Lord Jesus (Murray)...................................29

The Lord Jesus (Norbert) 30

The Mass is ended (Easter Alleluia) 162

The royal banners forward go 88

The stone which the builders rejected................176

There is no greater love....................................34

This day was made by the Lord (Dean).............172

This day was made by the Lord (Kielty) 174

This is wood of the Cross (Inwood) 62

This is wood of the Cross (Jordan).............60 & 61

This is wood of the Cross (Murray)....................60

Though one with God 20

Trisagion..79

Ubi caritas (Plainsong).....................................41

Ubi caritas (Taizé) 38

Veronica's Litany 110

Vexilla regis..89

Victimae paschali laudes (Plainsong) 181

Victimae paschali laudes (Steel) 184

Vidi aquam 166

Vous qui pleurez..86

What have they done to you, Lord?...................110

What wondrous love 109

When I survey 112

When the people heard......................................11

Where is love...40

With joy you will draw water (Forrester) 147

With joy you will draw water (Jordan)...............148

With joy you will draw water (Murray)............148

You have the message (Davis)...........................151

You have the message (Jordan)..........................149

You have the message (Murray) 151

You, Lord, have the message (Inwood) 149

You who mourn..86